GEORGIA

MORE DAILY DEVOTIONS FOR DIE-HARD FANS

BULLDOGS

MORE GEORGIA

More Daily Devotions for Die-Hard Fans: Georgia Bulldogs
© 2013 Ed McMinn
Extra Point Publishers; P.O. Box 871; Perry, GA 31069

Library of Congress Cataloging-in-Publication Data
13 ISBN Digit ISBN: 978-0-9882595-3-9

Manufactured in the United States of America.

Visit us at www.die-hardfans.com.

Cover and interior design by Slynn McMinn.

Every effort has been made to identify copyright holders. Any omissions are unintentional. Extra Point Publishers should be notified in writing immediately for full acknowledgement in future editions.

BULLDOGS

To
My Bulldog son, David,
and his Bullpup sons,
Jason and Brandon

A Note from the Author

This is actually Volume II of *Daily Devotions for Die-Hard Fans: Georgia Bulldogs*. The devotions and their stories are all new, written for this book. As with the first volume (which is still available), my hope is that you enjoy this humble offering. My prayer is that it in some way proves beneficial to you in your faith life.

-- Ed McMinn

The following titles are available:

DAY 1

AMAZING!

Read: Luke 4:31-36.

"All the people were amazed and said to each other, 'What is this teaching? With authority and power he gives orders to evil spirits and they come out!'" (v. 36)

It's amazing what our guys have done." So declared head coach Mark Richt after the 2006 Chick-fil-A Bowl. He was right.

The Dogs were solid underdogs to 14th-ranked Virginia Tech in the Dec.-30 game in Atlanta, and in the first half they were routed. Tech led 21-3, essentially leaving no doubts about the outcome. After all, the Hokies had the best total defense in college ball and had given up only five last-half touchdowns all season.

So what Georgia pulled off in the final thirty minutes of the game was amazing. The second half started like more of the same: Georgia punted. On their second possession, though, the Dogs at least managed a 51-yard field goal from Brandon Coutu. 21-6.

Then came the play that turned the momentum around for the rest of the night: The Dogs pulled off a successful onside kick. A few plays later, freshman Matthew Stafford hit tight end Martrez Milner with a 6-yard touchdown toss. Suddenly and amazingly, Georgia was only one score behind at 21-13.

The score stayed the same until early in the fourth quarter. When linebacker Tony Taylor, the game's defensive MVP, picked off a Tech pass, the Dogs attacked. They covered 43 yards in four plays with Kregg Lumpkin scoring from the 3. A Milner reception for the two-point conversion amazingly tied the game.

But the Dawgs weren't through. Tech fumbled on the first play after the kickoff, and Georgia got a Coutu field goal out of the deal to lead 24-21. After the kickoff, Taylor grabbed his second interception and returned it 16 yards to the Hokie 1. Fullback Brannan Southerland bulled his way into the end zone from there. Tech managed only a field goal after that, and Georgia had one of the most amazing wins in its history: 31-24.

The word "amazing" defines the limits of what you believe to be plausible or usual. The Grand Canyon, the birth of your children, a Bulldog comeback from certain defeat -- they're amazing! You've never seen anything like that before!

Some people in Galilee felt the same way when they encountered Jesus. Jesus amazed them with the authority of his teaching, and he wowed them with his power over spirit beings. People everywhere just couldn't quit talking about him.

It would have been amazing had they *not* been amazed. They were, after all, witnesses to the most amazing spectacle in the history of the world: God himself was right there among them walking, talking, teaching, preaching, and healing.

Their amazement should be a part of your life too because Jesus still lives. The almighty, omnipotent God of the universe seeks to spend time with you daily – because he loves you. Amazing!

It's amazing. That's Georgia; we never give up. We will never give up.
-- Defensive tackle Ray Gant after the Chick-fil-A Bowl

Everything about God is amazing, but perhaps
most amazing of all is that he loves us
and desires our company.

DAY 2

SOUND OFF!

Read Revelation 4:1-10, 5:6-14.

"Then I looked and heard the voice of many angels, numbering thousands upon thousands, and ten thousand times ten thousand" (v. 11a).

For the Bulldogs and their reliable kicker, the cannon's roar was not a cause for celebration.

The Dawgs of 1966 came within a conversion of an undefeated season and perhaps a national title, going 10-1 and losing only to Miami 7-6. The team won head coach Vince Dooley's first SEC title, clinching the championship at Auburn with a 21-13 win.

In the season finale, Bobby Dodd brought an undefeated Georgia Tech team into Athens for his last game as head coach. Tech led early 7-0, but Georgia rallied with a touchdown set up by a play the coaches had drawn up on the sideline. Halfback Kent Lawrence, who would be All-SEC in 1968, rushed onto the field with the play, a sweep that made a first down inside the Tech 10.

The touchdown that followed cut Tech's lead to 7-6 with the gimme conversion by Bobby Etter to follow. After all, the senior was such a sure thing that he led the SEC in scoring that season and had missed only two PATs his entire career. He was, however, in for a loud surprise.

In what turned out to be less than a stroke of brilliance, some overly enthusiastic fans had brought a cannon to the stadium to fire after each UGA touchdown. It went off prematurely, just as

Etter began to move through his kick. The roar of the discharge threw him off and he missed, leaving Tech with the 7-6 lead.

It didn't matter; the Dawgs dominated the rest of the game. Dooley emptied his bench in the last five minutes, which enabled Tech to score and make the final a deceptively close 23-14.

And the malefic cannon? At a ceremony the next week, it was embedded in concrete and dropped into the Chattahoochee River.

Sanford Stadium erupts in a cacophony on game day. Loud music blares from the rattling speakers in the car next to you at the traffic light. The garbage men bang the cans around as though they receive bonuses for waking you up. A silence of any length in a conversation makes us uncomfortable; somebody please say something.

We live in a noisy world, which means activity, busyness, progress, and engagement with life. The problem with all that noise – however constructive it may be – is that it drowns out God's gentle voice. Thus, some quiet time each day is absolutely imperative if we are to grow our relationship with God. The intentional seeking of silence in which to hear God's voice constitutes surrender to the divine.

Though much about Heaven will be strange, we should be quite comfortable there. Revelation's lengthy description of God's home makes it very clear that it's a noisy place reverberating with the inspiring, exhilarating, and awesome sound of worship.

I was quite irritated.
-- Vince Dooley's understated reaction to the cannon fire

**Heaven is a quite noisy place, echoing constantly
with the wonderful sounds of worship.**

DAY 3

SOMETHING NEW

Read Ephesians 4:17-24.

"You were taught . . . to put off your old self . . . and to put on the new self, created to be like God in true righteousness and holiness" (vv. 22, 24).

Herschel Walker's impact on the football field has been well documented. He was also, however, indirectly involved in the launching of a new sports program at UGA.

With the recruiting war for Herschel raging full blast in the late 1970s, schools were frantically scrambling for any way they could to gain an edge. Georgia had a big one: Herschel's sister, Veronica. She was a year older than he and was a track and field star for Johnson County High School. UGA backfield coach Mike Cavan, who with recruiting director Steve Greer was in charge of recruiting Herschel, saw Veronica training one day. "She was as impressive as a girl athlete as Herschel was as a guy," Cavan said.

Terror struck, though, when the Johnson Co. High track coach told Cavan that Clemson and Tennessee had offered Veronica a track scholarship. Cavan immediately called Vince Dooley. "Do you suppose that if we sign her, we will get Herschel?" his boss asked. "It's not 100 percent, but it couldn't hurt us," Cavan replied.

There was only one problem, and it was a big one. UGA didn't have a women's track and field program. When Cavan mentioned this slight drawback to Dooley, the coach's answer was concise and simple. "We'll just start [one]," he said.

BULLDOGS

Actually, it was already in the works as UGA implemented new women's programs under pressure from Title IX. "I would have to say we moved the plan up a year," Dooley said.

So Veronica Walker inaugurated a new program as the first-ever female to receive a track and field scholarship from UGA. As Dooley later put it, Veronica "was a tremendous athlete in her own right." Indeed. She was All-America in 1982 in the outdoor 100-meter dash.

New things in our lives often have a life-changing effect. A new spouse, for instance. A new baby. A new job. A new sports team in Athens. Even something as mundane as a new television set or a new lawn mower jolts us with change.

While new experiences, new people, and new toys may make our lives new, they can't make new lives for us. Inside, where it counts – down in the deepest recesses of our soul – we're still the same, no matter how desperately we may wish to change.

An inner restlessness drives us to seek escape from a life that is a monotonous routine. Such a mundane existence just isn't good enough for someone who is a child of God; it can't even be called living. We want more out of life; something's got to change.

The only hope for a new life lies in becoming a brand new man or woman. And that is possible only through Jesus Christ, he who can make all things new again.

One of the things I used to pray for every night was for God to let me beat Veronica.
-- Herschel Walker on outrunning his sister in junior high

A brand new you with the promise of a life worth living is waiting in Jesus Christ.

DAY 4

HIDEAWAY

Read Psalm 139:1-12.

"Where can I go from your Spirit? Where can I flee from your presence?" (v. 7)

Some Bulldogs intent on a little partying thought they could hide their plans from their coaches. They wound up trapped with the evidence.

The 1971 Dogs went 10-1 and earned a berth in the Gator Bowl. Mac McWhorter, an All-SEC guard and team captain in 1973, recalled that head coach Vince Dooley really wanted to win the bowl game since it was a match-up against his brother, Bill, at North Carolina. Thus, Dooley stuck his team in a hotel "way out of town and didn't let us have cars or anything."

McWhorter and some teammates decided one night to throw themselves a party anyway. They rounded up a big suitcase, took a cab to a package store, packed the case with beer, and then iced the beer down in the case.

Pleased with their stealth, the boys punched the elevator button at the hotel, the last step in their escapade. To their horror, when the door opened, they stood face-to-face with Dooley, Erk Russell, assistant coach Pat Hodgson, and their wives. Despite the players' earnest protestations, the group politely insisted that they join them for the ride up. Nobody said anything about the suitcase even though by now water was dripping from it.

To the players' relief, the coaches' floor came first, and they

BULLDOGS

exited. "You boys have fun," Russell remarked on the way out. As the door began to close, McWhorter and his teammates relaxed, figuring they had gotten away with it. Suddenly, though, a big hand with a cigar in it blocked the door. Russell looked right at McWhorter and said, "One more thing, Mac. Next time you go wash your clothes, make sure to dry them before putting them back into the suitcase." Then he smiled and let the door shut.

Like Mac McWhorter and his fellow Bulldogs, we often believe we can hide what we're doing from others. You may have had a hideout when you were a child. You may have a place in your home that's all yours, a spot where you can hide for a brief time and enjoy the solitude of hiding from the world. But even in that hideout and even in that personal place, you are not and never have been alone. God is there.

We do and believe many foolish things over the course of our lives, but little is as ridiculous as believing we can hide from God or that God won't notice what we're doing, saying, or thinking.

Here's the bad news: God is omnipresent; he is everywhere, all the time. We can't hide from him.

On the other hand, here's the good news: God is omnipresent; he is everywhere, all the time. We can't hide from him. God, thus, is always with us, and so is his comforting presence, his boundless love, and his saving grace.

God sees, God knows, God loves.

We hadn't gotten away with anything.
-- Mac McWhorter after Erk Russell's admonition

We can't hide from God's presence, which means
we also can't escape his love and his grace.

DAY 5

THOSE THINGS

Read Luke 13:1-9.

"Or those eighteen who died when the tower in Siloam fell on them -- do you think they were more guilty than all the others living in Jerusalem? I tell you, no!" (vv 4, 5a)

A series of "those things" kept Marlon Brown from being the star at Georgia he hoped he would be, but the bad breaks never changed his conviction that he was a blessed man.

A 5-star recruit, Brown was the first private-school player in Memphis history to be named a *Parade* All-America. He was Tennessee's Mr. Football as a senior in 2008, and the Dawgs pulled off a recruiting coup by nabbing him. He was 6-5 and weighed 230 lbs.; he would be a star.

But it just never happened. A combination of injuries, circumstances, and competition kept Brown from blossoming into the Bulldogs' ace receiver. He never even made All-SEC honorable mention or had 500 receiving yards in a season.

In his senior season of 2012, though, it all seemed to come together for him. He stood on the verge of a break-out year until another of "those things" rose up. This one was the cruelest blow of all; it ended his collegiate career.

On Nov. 3, in the third quarter against Ole Miss, Brown made his third catch of the day, bringing his total to 113 yards for the game. That also upped his totals for the season to 27 catches for 469 yards, an average of 17.4 yards per reception, making Brown

BULLDOGS

a legitimate deep threat.

When a defensive back crashed into his left knee after he made that reception against Ole Miss, Brown knew he was hurt. He didn't think it was serious, just a little sprain maybe. But it was a torn ACL. He would not play another down for the Dogs.

It was just one of those things.

You've probably had a few of "those things" in your own life: bad breaks that occur without regard to justice, morality, or fair play. You wonder if maybe everything in life is random with events determined by a chance roll of some cosmic dice. Is there really somebody scripting all this with logic and purpose?

Yes, there is; God is the author of everything.

We know how it all began; we even know how it all will end. It's in God's book. The part we play in God's kingdom, though, is in the middle, and that part is still being revealed. The simple truth is that God's ways are different from ours. After all he's God and we are not. That's why we don't know what's coming our way, and why "those things" in our lives catch us by surprise and dismay us when they do occur.

What God asks of us is that we trust him. As the one – and the only one – in charge, he knows everything will be all right for those who follow Jesus.

Never unlucky, never unfortunate. Things happen in life. I'm very blessed to be at the University of Georgia. I just roll with the punches.
-- Marlon Brown on 'those things'

Life confounds us because, while we know the end and the beginning of God's great story, we are part of the middle, which God is still writing.

THE LAST WORD

Read Luke 9:22-27.

"The Son of Man . . . must be killed and on the third day be raised to life. . . . [S]ome who are standing here will . . . see the kingdom of God" (vv. 22, 27).

Andy Landers first had some words of encouragement for his players and later some words of instruction. Jasmine James, however, had the last word, and the Lady Bulldogs were still dancing in March.

The sixth-seeded Dawgs were underdogs when they went up against third-seeded FSU on March 22 in the second round of the 2011 NCAA tournament. In the last half, the game seemed to be unwinding exactly as the tournament seedings indicated when FSU led 51-41 with about ten minutes left.

During a time out, Landers talked his team up. "Coach said some things to fire us up," said Anne Marie Armstrong, a guard/forward who would be ·All-SEC as a junior in 2011-12. Landers "said it wasn't over, and we picked things up defensively. Things really changed for us after that."

Indeed they did. The Dogs went on a 14-2 run capped by a pair of jumpers from junior guard Meredith Mitchell. The teams then swapped points for a while as the clock ticked away.

The Noles hit a free throw with 34 seconds left to take a 59-58 lead. With only 10 seconds left, the Dogs missed a shot, but Mitchell forced a jump ball with the possession arrow going the

BULLDOGS

Dogs' way.

During a time out, Landers reminded his team that everybody should get on the boards. With four seconds left, the team missed another shot but James, a guard who stands all of 5' 9", snared the rebound and nailed the putback with 2.9 seconds left. She was fouled, hit the free throw, and had the last word in UGA's dramatic 61-59 upset win. The team moved on to the Sweet 16.

Why is it that we often come up with the last word – the perfect zinger -- only long after the incident that called for a smart and pithy rejoinder is over? "Man, I shoulda said that! That woulda fixed his wagon!" But it's too late.

Nobody in history, though, including us, could ever hope to match the man who had the greatest last word of them all: Jesus Christ. His enemies killed him and put him in a tomb, confident they were done with that nuisance for good. Pontius Pilate, the Jewish religious leaders, the Roman soldiers, the people just out to watch a spectacle -- they all thought it was all said and done. Instead, they were unwitting participants in God's great plan of redemption and gave the last word to Jesus. He has it still.

Jesus didn't go to that cross so he could die; he went to that cross so all those who follow him might live. Because of Jesus' own death on the cross, the final word for us is not our own death. Rather it is life, through our salvation in Jesus Christ.

When the shot went up, I was able to get to the boards and knock the shot in.

-- Jasmine James on the last word against FSU

**With Jesus, the last word is
always life and never death.**

DAY 7

UNBELIEVABLE!

Read Hebrews 3:7-19.

"See to it, brothers, that none of you has a sinful, unbelieving heart that turns away from the living God" (v. 12).

The play was so unbelievable that the opposing quarterback turned to the ref to make sure it really happened.

When the Dawgs traveled to Columbia for the second game of the 2002 season, No. 47 was a complete unknown, a sophomore with "decent if subdued expectations." Those early expectations were at fullback -- thus, his jersey number.

But in the August scrimmages, "the kid was aggressive, flashy, a hard worker with surprising quickness." His intensity inevitably sent him to the defensive side of the ball, and his quickness off the snap made him an end. On Sept. 14, the game against the Gamecocks turned out to be "the coming-out party of [this] three-time All-American." He was David Pollack.

David Greene hit wide receiver Fred Gibson down the sideline for a 52-yard bomb, and Billy Bennett booted a field goal for a 3-0 Georgia lead. After a weather delay, Pollack threw his party.

For the night, he had eight tackles, two for loss. He also had a fumble recovery, a pass deflection, and a rush that panicked the Gamecock quarterback into an ill-fated pitch that sealed the 13-7 win for the Dawgs when Thomas Davis fell on the loose ball.

And then there was that unbelievable play. It came with UGA

holding onto that 3-0 lead, and USC trying to pass from its own end zone. The quarterback drew back to pass, and then "by some sleight of hand that even seemed to fool the television camera," the ball wound up in Pollack's arms. He had lifted the ball from the quarterback's hand at the moment it came out.

The ref signalled for a touchdown on a play officially ruled as an interception. The bewildered USC quarterback turned to the official and asked, "Are you serious?" He couldn't believe it either.

Much of what taxes the limits of our belief system has little effect on our lives. Maybe we don't believe in UFOs, honest politicians, aluminum baseball bats, Sasquatch, or the viability of electric cars. A healthy dose of skepticism is a natural defense mechanism that helps protect us in a world that all too often has designs on taking advantage of us.

That's not the case, however, when Jesus and God are part of the mix. Quite unbelievably, we often hear people blithely assert they don't believe in God. Or brazenly declare they believe in God but don't believe Jesus was anything but a good man and a great teacher.

At this point, unbelief becomes dangerous because God doesn't fool around with scoffers. He locks them out of the Promised Land, which isn't a country in the Middle East but Heaven itself.

Given that scenario, it's downright unbelievable that anyone would not believe.

Football is so incredible sometimes it's unbelievable.

-- Tom Landry

Perhaps nothing is as unbelievable as that some people insist on not believing in God or his son.

UNBELIEVABLE!   17

DAY 8

CONFIDENCE MAN

Read Micah 7:5-7.

"As for me, I will look to the Lord, I will wait for the God of my salvation" (v. 7 NRSV).

Blair Walsh's self-confidence took a beating his senior season, but it received a big boost against Kentucky when he booted the Dawgs into the SEC Championship Game.

In his final game as Georgia's kicker, the 2012 Outback Bowl, Walsh set the all-time SEC scoring record with 412 points, breaking the record of 409 points set by former Bulldog kicker Billy Bennett. Walsh was nothing short of sensational his sophomore and junior seasons; in 2009, he hit 20 of 22 field goals, and as a junior, he nailed 20 of 23 kicks.

The 2011 season, however, was one long struggle for the senior kicker as he hit only 21 of 35 field goals. At one point, he was so frustrated he threw his helmet into a trash can. Head coach Mark Richt eventually let junior backup Brandon Bogotay battle Walsh for the job. That didn't help Walsh's confidence, but neither did the results. Bogotay held his own, and Richt went with a rotation.

Walsh confessed that his struggles shook the self-confidence a successful kicker absolutely must have. At one point, he admitted he would be lying if he said otherwise.

Then came the Kentucky game of Nov. 19. The Saturday morning of the game, Richt decided to go with Walsh because he felt the kicker was "extremely hot." He was.

BULLDOGS

With a win over Kentucky, the Dawgs won the SEC East; a loss sent South Carolina to the title showdown. Unfortunately, the UGA offense never really got going; fortunately, Walsh's foot did.

Walsh confidently hit four field goals in four attempts, single-handedly outscoring Kentucky in the 19-10 win. He said after the game, "Your team giving you high-fives because you made [the kicks] and not trying to console you because you missed them made it feel like old times today." The excitement reminded Walsh of those days when he was a confident kicker.

You need confidence in all areas of your life. You're confident the company you work for will pay you on time, or you wouldn't go to work. You turn the ignition confident your car will start. When you flip a switch, you expect the light to come on.

Confidence in other people and in things is often misplaced, though. Companies go broke; car batteries die; light bulbs burn out. Even the people you love the most sometimes let you down.

So where can you place your trust with absolute confidence you won't be betrayed? In the promises of God.

Such confidence is easy, of course, when everything's going your way, but what about when you cry as Micah did, "What misery is mine!" As Micah says, that's when your confidence in God must be its strongest. That's when you wait for the Lord confident that God will not fail you, that he will never let you down.

When it gets right down to the wood-chopping, the key to winning is confidence.

-- Legendary college football coach Darrell Royal

People, things, and organizations will let you down; only God can be trusted confidently.

DAY 9

STORY TIME

Read Luke 8:26-39.

"'Return home and tell how much God has done for you.'
So the man went away and told all over town how much
Jesus had done for him" (v. 39).

From an answered prayer to a unique kickoff in the Sugar Bowl, Rex Robinson has some stories to tell from his days at UGA.

Robinson is a true Bulldog legend, a two-time All-American kicker (1979 and 1980). Over the years, he has frequently been asked, "Are you *the* Rex Robinson?" It has happened so often that a bunch of his coworkers nicknamed him "The."

Perhaps Robinson's most exciting moment came with the kick that beat Kentucky for the Wonderdawgs of 1978. Georgia rallied from a 16-0 deficit to trail 16-14 and drove to the Wildcat 10 with a handful of seconds left. Robinson was calmly going through his set routine when Kentucky called a time out to ice him.

That turned out to be fortunate for the Dawgs. Tim Morrison, who was supposed to be in the game blocking, was kneeling on the sidelines praying. Head coach Vince Dooley leaned over him and said, "Your prayers have just been answered. Kentucky called timeout." Prayers all across the Bulldog Nation were answered when Robinson nailed the kick for the 17-16 win.

In the 1981 Sugar Bowl, Robinson's job was to kick off high and away from the better of Notre Dame's two return men. After he tied the game at 3-3 late in the first quarter, he did indeed sail one high. Both Notre Dame players ran away from the ball, and UGA's Bob Kelly recovered it to set up an easy Herschel-Walker touchdown. Defensive coordinator Erk Russell called Robinson's boot "the longest onside kick in history."

That season, Robinson missed the Buck-Belue-to-Lindsay-Scott miracle in Jacksonville. When Scott got to midfield on the play, Robinson ran to the end of the bench to get his tee, figuring he would have to kick a game-winning field goal. By the time he got back to the sideline, Scott was being mobbed in the end zone.

Yep, Rex Robinson has a story or two to tell, just as you do. It's the story of your life and it's unique. No one else among the billions of people on this planet can tell the same story.

Part of that story is your encounter with Jesus. It's the most important chapter of all, but, strangely enough, believers in Jesus Christ often don't tell it. Otherwise brave and daring Christian men and women who wouldn't think twice of skydiving or white-water rafting often quail when they are faced with the prospect of speaking about Jesus to someone else. It's the dreaded "W" word: witness. "I just don't know what to say," they sputter.

But witnessing is nothing but telling your story. No one can refute it; no one can claim it isn't true. You don't get into some great theological debate for which you're ill prepared. You just tell the beautiful, awesome story of Jesus and you.

My wife is from Michigan, teaching with people who make a big deal about it when they find out we're married. She thinks it's really funny.
-- Rex Robinson as his Bulldog story continues

We all have a story to tell, but the most important part of all is the chapter where we meet Jesus.

DAY 10

UNCERTAIN TIMES

Read Psalm 18:1-6, 20-29.

"The Lord is my rock . . . in whom I take refuge. He is my shield, and the horn of my salvation, my stronghold" (v. 2).

In one painful moment, gymnast Kaylan Earls' life was suddenly filled with uncertainty.

Earls knew nothing about injury. In high school, she was twice the Junior Olympic National All-Around Champion. Her body seemed impervious to the demands her sport placed upon it. Whatever she wanted to do that involved gymnastics, she just did it and she did it exceptionally well -- until Dec. 30, 2010, about two weeks before the collegiate gymnastics season began. That's when, Earls, a Bulldog freshman, blew out her left Achilles tendon during practice. "I was on floor tumbling and took off and it snapped right there," she recalled.

She was instantly in a place she'd never been before and didn't know how to react. "I freaked out," she admitted. She first tried to get up and walk it off. Coach Jay Clark had been through a similar injury suffered by All-American Courtney Kupets in 2008, so he knew what to do. He rushed over and told Earls not to move.

Earls underwent surgery, and that's when the real uncertainty began. She realized early on that the hardest part of her rehab would be rebuilding the certainty she had had in her body's ability to do what she demanded of it. Clark described her situation as being "a little gun-shy."

Earls' reaction was understandable. Inactivity after her surgery resulted in the loss of much of the muscle mass in her left foot and ankle. Her first order of business was to rebuild her strength. Only later came the rebuilding of her confidence.

She did, though. After missing the 2011 season, Earls was the regular season beam MVP in 2012, setting a personal high of 9.9. The uncertainty long behind her, she was in the Dawgs beam and floor lineup in 2013 and earned SEC honors for excellence.

Even when we believe UGA will field another great gymnastics or football team, we have some uncertainty because nothing in sport is a sure thing. If it were, it wouldn't be any fun.

Life is like that. We never know what's in store for us or what's going to happen next. We can be riding high one day with a job promotion, good health, a nice family, and sunny weather. Only a short time later, we can be unemployed, sick, divorced, and/or broke. When we place our trust in life itself and its rewards, we are certain to face uncertain times.

We must search out a haven, a place where we know we can find certainty to ease our trepidation and anxiety about life's uncertainties. We can find that haven, that rock, by dropping to our knees. There, we can find that certainty – every time.

Our life and times are uncertain. The Lord God Almighty is sure – and is only a prayer away.

I wanted to be the same and I didn't know. That was the tough part. I didn't know.
> -- *Kaylan Earls on the uncertainty after her injury*

Only God offers certainty amid life's uncertainty.

HEAD GAMES

Read Philippians 4:4-9.

"Do not be anxious about anything. . . . And the God of peace will be with you" (vv. 6a, 9b).

For Georgia to hang on and beat Florida, quarterback Aaron Murray was going to have to be tough. What was needed, though, was not physical toughness but mental resilience.

Despite all the gaudy stats that made him the greatest passer in Georgia football history late in his junior season, Murray still had one big black mark on his career: He lacked a signature win over a top-10 team. He had a chance to rectify that on Oct. 27, 2012, against the third-ranked Florida Gators.

So he promptly went out and had his most miserable start ever, throwing interceptions on three straight first-half drives. The third pick resulted from what Murray called "probably the worst throw I've ever made in my life."

Obviously, if Georgia was going to win, Murray had to fight his way back from his horrendous start. He would need the mental toughness not to lose faith in himself and to continue to believe he could make the plays his team needed.

His coaches believed in him. With the defense shutting the Gators down, Georgia led 7-6 at halftime. Offensive coordinator Mike Bobo told his beleaguered quarterback that they were not going to abandon the passing game. "You're going to have to win this ballgame," the coach said.

BULLDOGS

Bobo was true to his word. In the fourth quarter with Georgia clinging to a 10-9 lead, the game was put in Murray's hands. He responded with a scoring drive that featured pass plays on six of seven snaps. The last one was a 45-yard touchdown toss to Malcolm Mitchell, the record-setting 76th of Murray's career. The play put the final of 17-9 on the scoreboard.

Murray had his signature win, achieved in large part because he was mentally tough enough to fight and to persevere.

Once upon a time, survival required mere brute strength, but persevering in American society today generally necessitates mental strength rather than physical prowess.

Your job, your family, your finances -- they all demand mental toughness from you by placing stress upon you to perform. Stress is a fact of life, though it isn't all bad as we are often led to believe. Stress can lead you to function at your best. Rather than buckling under it, you stand up, make constant decisions, and keep going.

So it is with your faith life. "Too blessed to be stressed" sounds nice, but followers of Jesus Christ know all about stress. Society screams compromise; your children whine about being cool; your company ignores ethics. But you don't fold beneath the stress; you keep your mind on Christ and the way he said to live because you are tough mentally, strengthened by your faith.

After all, you have God's word and God's grace for relief and support. Pray, trust, and relax.

A bad start is a test of a guy's toughness at the quarterback position.
-- Mark Richt on Aaron Murray's start vs. Florida

**Toughened mentally by your faith in Christ,
you live out what you believe, and you persevere.**

DAY 12

PAYBACK

Read Matthew 5:38-42.

"I tell you, Do not resist an evil person. If someone strikes you on the right cheek, turn to him the other also" (v. 39).

It took fifteen years, but the Dogs finally exacted some revenge for one of the most disappointing losses in school history.

In 1927, the Bulldogs were undefeated, untied, and ranked No. 1 with a Rose Bowl bid all but in the bag when Tech upset them 12-0 in the mud at Grant Field. In 1942, Tech was 9-0 and the Bulldogs were 9-1. To the winner went the SEC title and the Rose Bowl.

The pregame publicity for the '42 game was the biggest since that 1927 clash. Thousands of extra seats were built at Sanford Stadium. The *Atlanta Journal* declared, "[E]arly in the morning, the invasion of Athens began and every road leading into the beautiful university city groaned beneath the load" as thousands of people "began arriving in automobiles whose rationed gas had been saved for months." Forty-two thousand fans jammed into Sanford, the largest crowd in the state's sports history.

Tech was not ready for what the Bulldogs unleashed on them: the backfield combo of Heisman-Trophy winner Frank Sinkwich and future All-America Charley Trippi. Sinkwich set up Georgia's first score with an interception. Three plays later, Trippi passed to end Van Davis for a 17-yard touchdown. Leo Costa booted the conversion, which set an all-time collegiate scoring record. He scored in every game of his four-year career at Georgia. Of course, no one knew it at the game, but a full-fledged rout was on.

The Dawgs drove 92 yards on their next possession to lead 14-0 early in the second quarter. Later in the period, Trippi dropped back to pass and took off when he couldn't find anybody open. He went 87 yards, still the longest Bulldog run in the series, and Georgia led 20-0. The UGA band struck up "California, Here I Come" while the Bulldog fans started celebrating early.

The Dogs won 34-0, securing their long-overdue revenge by squashing Tech's national-title and Rose-Bowl hopes.

The very nature of an intense rivalry is that the loser will seek payback for the defeat of the season before. But what about in life when somebody's done you wrong; is it time to get even?

The problem with revenge in real-life is that it isn't as clear-cut as a scoreboard. Life is so messy that any attempt at revenge is often inadequate or, worse, backfires and injures you.

As a result, you remain gripped by resentment and anger, which hurts you and no one else. You poison your own happiness while that other person goes blithely about her business. The only way someone who has hurt you can keep hurting you is if you're a willing participant.

But it doesn't have to be that way. Jesus ushered in a new way of living when he taught that we are not to seek revenge for personal wrongs and injuries. Let it go and go on with your life. What a relief!

Georgia is the greatest team in the country.
-- Tech head coach Bobby Dodd after the '42 game

Resentment over a wrong injures you, not the other person, so forget it -- just as Jesus taught.

DAY 13

ACT NATURAL

Read Matthew 7:13-23.

"Not everyone who says to me, 'Lord, Lord,' will enter the kingdom of heaven" (v. 21a).

Zach Cone often used his bat to benefit the Diamond Dogs. Once, though, his acting skills helped get a win.

After his junior season in 2011, Cone was drafted in the first round by the Texas Rangers and turned pro. His best year as a Dog was 2010, when he won the team's triple crown with a .363 average, 10 home runs, and 53 RBI's. In 2011, he was perfect in the outfield, handling 161 chances without an error.

On May 1, 2011, neither Cone's hitting nor his fielding chased the winning run home. The Razorbacks from Arkansas led 5-3 in the bottom of the ninth, but the Dawgs put together a rally. Sophomore Brett DeLoach, the designated hitter, led off with a double. Pinch hitter Chase Davidson was nailed by a pitch and went to first with the tying run.

Freshman centerfielder Conor Welton moved the runners up with a sacrifice bunt. Junior outfielder Peter Verdin then lined a single to chase both runners home and tie the game up. Arkansas intentionally walked second-baseman Levi Hyams, the team's leading hitter, who had smashed a two-run homer earlier in the game. After a strikeout, a walk to shortstop Kyle Farmer loaded the bases and set the stage for an anti-climactic finish.

The first pitch to Cone caught just enough of his hand to merit some attention from the umpire. "I thought [the umpire] was going to call a foul ball at first, the way he was signaling," Verdin said. Until Cone helped the ump out with some exaggerated hand flipping as if he were in extreme pain from the plunking.

He got the call, and Verdin trotted home with the winning run.

Acting like a Christian – even if we're as good at acting as Zach Cone was – won't help any of us walk through the gates of Heaven. In other words, we can't fake being a follower of Jesus; well, we can, but it won't do us any good. That's because Jesus will see right through our deception to our heart, where the truth lies.

So what's the difference between a true follower of Jesus and a faker? With a good actor, only two people really know: Jesus and the person. Somebody may be all over town all the time doing these great and noble deeds for everyone. Only in that person's heart, though, lies the truth. Is all that good work being done for self-gratification or out of love and for God's glory? If it's the former, then it's all acting; it isn't real. It's hypocritical.

Doing God's will and not our own is all that matters, for that is the mission Christians are called to. We can discern that mission from only one source, Jesus himself. In following Jesus, we thus live a true life, not a fake one; we live the life that God intends for us. We don't act at being Christians. Then when this life is ended, we walk through that straight and narrow gate. For real.

Zach shook his hand good. I don't know if it hit him or not, but it looked like it did.
                    -- Peter Verdin on Zach Cone's ninth-inning histrionics

**If what we're doing isn't God's will for our lives,
then we are merely acting at being Christians.**

DAY 14

A FAST START

Read Acts 2:40-47.

*"Everyone was filled with awe. . . . [They] ate together
with glad and sincere hearts, praising God and enjoying
the favor of all the people" (vv. 43a, 46b, 47a).*

Todd Gurley got off to quite a fast start as a Bulldog.

As a true freshman running back in 2012, Gurley rushed for
1,385 yards with 17 touchdowns, the latter a Bulldog freshman
record. He led all SEC running backs in rushing, finishing second
in the league to Texas A&M's Heisman-Trophy winner, Johnny
Manziel. Gurley is the second true freshman in Georgia history
to rush for 1,000 yards; the other is Herschel Walker (1980). He
was named First-Team All-SEC by the Associated Press and was
named to several freshman All-America teams.

Gurley didn't actually get off to a fast start among those who
followed UGA's recruiting effort. That honor belonged to another
outstanding freshman on the 2012 team, fellow running back
and North Carolinian Keith Marshall. Rated the nation's No.-1
running back by several recruiting services, Marshall got off
to a fast start in Athens, too. He rushed for 759 yards in 2012,
averaging a sensational 6.5 yards per carry.

In fact, Marshall signed with the Dawgs before Gurley did.
What few folks knew was that the two had agreed to sign with
the same school.

So when the Dogs opened the 2012 season at home against

BULLDOGS

Buffalo, much of the buzz was about Marshall and deservedly so. But it was Gurley who got off to the fast start.

On Georgia's opening series, Gurley gained one yard on his first carry. His second tote was a little better; he broke a tackle for a 10-yard touchdown run. Then came the real bomb. The next time he touched the ball, he gathered in a kickoff at the goal line, burst into the clear at the 20, and headed up the sideline. He went 100 yards for a touchdown. Three touches, two TDs. Fast start.

Fast starts are crucial for more than football games and races. Any time we begin something new, we want to get out of the gate quickly and jump ahead of the pack and stay there. We desire to build momentum from a fast start and keep rolling.

This is true for our faith life also. For a time after we accepted Christ as our savior, we were on fire with a zeal that wouldn't let us rest, much like the early Christians described in Acts. All too many Christians, however, let that blaze die down until only old ashes remain. We become lukewarm pew sitters.

The Christian life shouldn't be that way. Just because we were tepid yesterday doesn't mean we can't be boiling today. Every day we can turn to God for a spiritual tune-up that will put a new spark in our faith life; with a little tending that spark can soon become a raging fire. Today could be the day our faith life gets off to a fast start – again.

I didn't think it would be like this, maybe a touchdown, maybe 30 yards or something like that.
-- Todd Gurley after his fast start against Buffalo

**Every day offers us yet another chance
to get off to a fast start for Jesus.**

DAY 15

LIKE CLOCKWORK

Read Matthew 25:1-13.

"Keep watch, because you do not know the day or the hour" (v. 13).

In one of the most bizarre endings ever to a Georgia football game, the Bulldogs helped the clock run out on Auburn.

Approaching the Auburn game of 1992, the Dawgs were 7-2 and ranked 12th in the nation. With quarterback Eric Zeier, running back Garrison Hearst, receiver Andre Hastings, and tackle Alec Millen, the Dog offense was the seventh best in the country. Only a pair of losses by a total of five points kept the team from a possible shot at the national title.

On Nov. 14 in Auburn, the two squads played to a 7-7 tie in a defensive first half. Early in the second half, though, Zeier let fly with a 64-yard TD bomb to Hearst for a 14-7 Bulldog lead. Auburn cut the margin to 14-10 and was driving late when cornerback Al Jackson bailed the Dogs out with an interception in the end zone.

But the offense couldn't run out the clock and punted with 2:36 left. Auburn quickly came roaring down the field and called its last time out with the ball at the UGA 5. A run was driven out of bounds inside the 1 with 19 seconds on the clock.

What followed remains the subject of controversy -- at least with Auburn fans. The ball was only about a foot from the goal line and a game-winning touchdown. The Auburn quarterback took the snap and moved to his left. The handoff was mishandled, though, and the ball popped into the air. In the mad scramble, Auburn retained possession. Apparently.

As both teams argued and pushed and shoved, Bulldog head coach Ray Goff was "frantically motioning and screaming for his players to stay down." That's because the clock was running. It kept running right on down to zero before the Dogs leisurely picked themselves up and before Auburn could line up and run another play.

The Dogs had killed the clock and saved a 14-10 win.

While we may pride ourselves on our time management, the truth is that we don't manage time; it manages us. Hurried and harried, we live by schedules that seem to have too much what and too little when. By setting the bedside alarm at night, we even let the clock determine how much down time we get. A life of leisure actually means one in which time is of no importance.

Every second of our life – all the time we have – is a gift from God, who dreamed up time in the first place. We would do well, therefore, to consider what God considers to be good time management. After all, Jesus himself warned us against mismanaging the time we have. From God's point of view, using our time wisely means being prepared at every moment for Jesus' return, which will occur -- well, only time will tell when.

Linebacker Mitch Davis admitted later that he purposely laid on an Auburn player so the Tigers could not line up and run another play.
— Writer Patrick Garbin on the finish of the '92 Auburn game

We mismanage our time when we fail to prepare for Jesus' return even though we don't know when that will be.

DAY 16

BROKEN DREAMS

Read Joel 2:28-32.

"I will pour out my Spirit on all people. . . . Your old men will dream dreams" (v. 28).

What in the world had happened to his dreams?

In a gloomy, deserted bar on a Sunday morning, a 25-year-old man, "a good-looking fellow with an athletic build and empty eyes," went through the meaningless motions of cleaning up the joint. Only a few hours before, the place had been packed and boisterous. Mostly young people -- many of them his age -- had met friends and swapped stories and told lies. Many of them had good jobs and at least somewhat promising careers.

And here he was, "crawl[ing] on his hands and knees, wiping at something sticky on the carpet" and picking up the remains of snack nuts ground into that same carpet. His life had been reduced to "clean[ing] up the debris of other people's enjoyment."

Oh, he had once had dreams. In high school, he had been so cocky and so sure of himself that when his head coach asked him if he believed in God, he replied, "I don't know if I believe in God, but I know one thing. I sure believe in football."

But his life peaked in high school. After that, only disappointed hopes and shattered dreams followed. Alone that morning, his life as empty as the beer cans in the trash he had to take out, he recalled a story he had often heard about another cocky young man. That guy had hit the road with some big plans and glorious dreams only to spend all his money and burn out young. He finally "came to the end of himself," feeding pigs a long way from anybody who loved him. So he went home.

In the bar that Sunday morning, the prodigal with his broken dreams decided it was time, too, for him to go home, at least metaphorically. So he got to his feet, tossed his rag away, and walked out. Somehow, he would get back into football.

That young man was Mark Richt.

We all have particular dreams. Perhaps to make a fortune, coach a big-time college football team, write the great American novel, start up a business, or find the perfect spouse. More likely than not, though, we gradually lose our hold on those dreams. They slip away from us as we surrender them to the reality and the pressures of everyday living.

But we also have general dreams. For world peace. For an end to hunger. That no child should ever again be afraid. These dreams we hold onto doggedly as if something inside us tells us that even though the world gets itself into a bigger mess every year, one day everything will be all right.

That's because it will be. God has promised a time when his spirit will rule the world. Jesus spoke of a time when he will return to claim his kingdom. In that day, our dreams of peace and plenty and the banishment of hate and want will be reality.

Our dreams based on God's promises will come true.

To achieve in sports you first have to have a dream, and then you must act on that dream.

-- Speed skater Dianne Holum

Dreams based on God's promises will come true.

LIVE ACTION

Read James 2:14-26.

"Faith by itself, if it is not accompanied by action, is dead"
(v. 17).

Missouri talked. Georgia played. Advantage Dawgs.

Prior to Missouri's first-ever SEC game on Sept. 8, 2012, against Georgia, a Tiger tackle delivered some of the most famous (or infamous) bulletin-board material of the season. He said he turned off Georgia's season-opening 45-23 win over Buffalo because it was "like watching Big Ten football. It's old man football."

Not surprisingly, the comment about the SEC in general and Georgia in particular playing "old man football" made its way back to the Southeast. Bulldog head coach Mark Richt laughed when told of the unfortunate remark. "Did he say old man?" the coach asked. Even Richt's mother reacted to the insult, calling up her son to hear what he thought about it. UGA quarterback Aaron Murray said the Dawgs tried to ignore the "old man football" aspersion, "but I think it was definitely a little added incentive."

And then came Saturday when the time for talk was over and the time for action started. The action spoke much louder than the words. The seventh-ranked old men from Athens went into a frenzied Columbia, took everything the Tigers could throw at them, and then rallied for a 41-20 stomping that introduced the new kids on the block to the reality of SEC football.

Missouri led 17-9 early in the third quarter before UGA took

control of the game, scoring touchdowns on its next two possessions: Murray to Tavarres King and Murray to Marlon Brown.
After that came the Jarvis Jones show. He grabbed an interception
to set up a 1-yard touchdown run by Todd Gurley and then caused
a fumble that preceded Ken Malcome's 6-yard score.

The Dawgs had let their play do all their talking, at least before
the game. In their raucous locker room after the win, Murray and
linebacker Christian Robinson jubilantly held up a board that
proclaimed "Grown Man Football."

Talk is cheap. Consider your neighbor or coworker who talks
without saying anything, who makes promises she doesn't keep,
who brags about his own exploits, who can always tell you how to
do something but never shows up for the work. Even in football,
speech without action just doesn't cut it.

That principle applies in the life of a person of faith too. Merely
declaring our faith isn't enough, however sincere we may be. It is
putting our faith into action that shouts to the world of the depth
of our commitment to Christ.

Even Jesus didn't just talk, though he certainly did his share
of preaching and teaching. Rather, his ministry was a virtual
whirlwind of activity. As he did, so are we to change the world by
doing. Anybody can talk about Jesus, but it is when we act for him
that we demonstrate how much we love him.

Jesus Christ is alive; so should our faith in him be.

*I don't know what he meant by that, but bottom line is we've got to get
after it and do what we do well.*
-- Mark Richt on the 'old man football' comment

Faith that does not reveal itself in action is dead.

PROBLEM CHILD

Read James 1:2-12.

"Blessed is the man who perseveres under trial, because when he has stood the test, he will receive the crown of life that God has promised to those who love him" (v. 12).

The emergence of Herschel Walker certainly solved one problem for the 1980 Bulldogs, but it created another: what to do with the player he replaced.

The 16-15 win over Tennessee in the season opener in which the heralded freshman scored two touchdowns amounted to a discovery that Walker could play tailback. After that one game, it was obvious he was the man.

But what about Donnie McMickens? He was a fifth-year senior tailback who had worked hard to earn the start against Tennessee. Head coach Vince Dooley called him "a good football player." But he had been beaten out. Certainly, there was no disgrace in giving way to one of the greatest athletes in history -- but there it was.

At practice Monday, McMickens' "jaw was down on the ground." As Dooley saw it, he "was not good for himself or good for us with his current attitude." The coaches agreed that McMickens was "ruining the morale of the team." He was a problem.

Determined not to lose McMickens, Dooley summoned the disappointed player to his office. He told McMickens that he had lost his starting spot but not to "any normal human. . . . You have to accept that, whether you like it or not. He is a better player."

Then Dooley moved on. "We need you on this football team," he said. "[W]e want you to be a starter on every special team we have. We need you. We really do."

McMickens went for it. He was so good that he was voted the special teams captain and the special teams MVP. "He became our best special teams player," declared center Hugh Nall.

Donnie McMickens was a problem only for the opposition.

Problems are such a ubiquitous feature of our lives that a whole day – twenty-four hours – without a single problem ranks right up there with a government without taxes and a Bulldog team that never, ever loses a game. We just can't even imagine it.

But that's life. Even Jesus had his share of problems, especially with his twelve-man staff. Jesus could have easily removed all problems from his daily walk, but what good would that have done us? Our goal is to become like Jesus, and we could never fashion ourselves after a man who didn't encounter job stress, criticism, loneliness, temptation, frustration, and discouragement.

Instead, Jesus showed us that when – not if – problems come, a person of faith uses them to get better rather than letting the problems use him to get bitter. We learn God-filled perseverance and patience as we develop and deepen our faith and our trust in God. Problems will pass; eternity will not.

I don't believe we would have won the national championship without him.

-- *Vince Dooley on Donnie McMickens*

**The problem with problems is that
we often let them use us and make us bitter
rather than using them to become better.**

DAY 19

WINNER'S CIRCLE

Read 1 John 5:1-12.

"Who is it that overcomes the world? Only he who believes that Jesus is the Son of God" (v. 5).

According to *Sports Illustrated*, they were "bad at everything but winning."

They were the 1959 Georgia Bulldogs. The season before they had won only two SEC games, finishing tenth in the conference. The '59 squad was pretty much the same team, "except for Theron Sapp, Riley Gunnels, Nat Dye and most of the other good players who had graduated." Head coach Wally Butts said he had so few good players "that he could put all of them in one car and drive to the next game."

And yet here they were on a glorious November afternoon in Sanford Stadium sitting only twenty yards away from winning the SEC championship by upsetting Auburn. They trailed 13-7 and faced fourth-and-13 with 30 seconds on the clock.

What happened has assumed mythological proportions among Bulldog fans, but it is true. Quarterback Fran Tarkenton drew a play up in the huddle in the grass and dirt. Tight end Bill Herron delayed and then sprinted for the left corner of the end zone. Bill Soberdash and halfback Fred Brown decoyed over the middle.

Tarkenton rolled to his right and then suddenly wheeled and lofted the ball back to his left. Herron cradled the ball to tie the game, and Durward Pennington booted the PAT for the 14-13 win.

BULLDOGS

How in the world? The "good" players were few, but it was their quality that made the difference: Tarkenton, Charlie Britt, Brown with his horrible knees, and fullback Bill Godfrey, who Butts called "absolutely the slowest runner I've ever seen," but who always got the yards the team needed.

They joined with a bunch of scrappers to transform themselves into what all great football teams aspire to be: winners.

Life itself, not just athletic events, is a competition. You vie against other job applicants. You seek admission to a college with a limited number of open spots. You compete against others for a date. Sibling rivalry is real; just ask your brother or sister.

Inherent in any competition or in any situation that involves wining and losing is an antagonist. You always have an opponent to overcome, even if it's an inanimate video game, a golf course, or even yourself.

Nobody wants to be numbered among life's losers. We recognize them when we see them, and perhaps mutter a prayer that says something like, "There but for the grace of God go I."

But one adversary will defeat us: Death will claim us all. We can turn the tables on this foe, though; we can defeat the grave. A victory is possible, however, only through faith in Jesus Christ. With Jesus, we have hope beyond death because we have life.

With Jesus, we win -- for all of eternity.

Up front were fellows like Larry Lancaster, Jimmy Vickers and [Bill] Herron, who were really no great shakes at anything but winning.
*   -- Sports Illustrated on the '59 Dawgs*

Death is the ultimate opponent;
Jesus is the ultimate victor.

DAY 20

CELEBRATION TIME

Read Luke 15:1-10.

"There is rejoicing in the presence of the angels of God over one sinner who repents" (v. 10).

On a night worthy of celebration, the Bulldog men's basketball team and its fans did just that, including one Dawg who kissed the "G" at center court.

On March 2, 2011, the Bulldogs achieved a coveted milestone. In their last home game of the season, they rolled over LSU 73-53 for their twentieth win of the season. The victory touched off a celebration among both the fans and the players.

The evening began amid a spirit of celebration as it was Senior Night with center Jeremy Price and forward Chris Barnes being honored. The players might have been as keyed up as the fans when the game started. They got off to a slow start against the underdog Tigers, falling behind 13-4 less than five minutes into the game. "I thought early emotion got the better part of us," said head coach Mark Fox.

They settled down, though, and outscored LSU 26-12 over the last fourteen minutes of the half to lead 30-25 at the break. The defense keyed the run; during one stretch, the Dawgs held the Tigers without a bucket for more than nine minutes. UGA then turned the game into a blowout the last half.

Guard Gerald Robinson led the scoring with 16 points; Dustin Ware dropped in 15 with junior guard Travis Leslie adding 14.

BULLDOGS

The victory left the men with a 20-9 record, the first time since the 2001-02 season the program had notched twenty wins. The romp also clinched a winning record in the SEC, a pair of milestones that virtually assured the Dawgs a spot in the NCAA Tournament. "I'd argue all day for our team," asserted Fox.

Walk-on Matt Bucklin and Price cooked up a little victory celebration for the occasion. As the pair had planned, Price dropped down and kissed the "G" at center court with 46 seconds on the game clock when he checked out of the lineup for the last time.

Georgia just whipped Florida. You got that new job or that promotion. You just held your newborn child in your arms. Life has those grand moments that call for celebration. You may jump up and down and scream in a wild frenzy at a Dawg game or share a quiet, sedate candlelight dinner at home -- but you celebrate.

Consider then a celebration that is beyond our imagining, one that fills every niche and corner of the very home of God and the angels. Imagine a celebration in Heaven, which also has its grand moments. Those grand moments are touched off when someone comes to faith in Jesus. Heaven itself rings with the joyous sounds of the singing and dancing of the celebrating angels. Even God rejoices when just one person – you or someone you have introduced to Christ -- turns to him.

When you said "yes" to Christ, you made the angels dance.

It's a big deal for our team. The 20 mark is pretty special.
-- Jeremy Price, celebrating the win over LSU

God himself joins the angels in heavenly celebration when even a single person turns to him through faith in Jesus.

DAY 21

NEVER TOO LATE

Read John 11:17-27, 38-44.

"'But, Lord," said Martha, . . . "he has been there four days.' Then Jesus said, 'Did I not tell you that if you believed, you would see the glory of God?'" (vv. 19b-40)

Rennie Curran learned it's never too late to go home.

In 2009, *Sporting News* tabbed Curran, a junior linebacker, the SEC's best hitter and "the most dominant defensive player in the game." He was first-team All-SEC in '09 after leading the league in tackles with 116. That was the highest total for a Bulldog since Orantes Grant had 120 stops in 1998. He passed on his senior season to enter the 2010 NFL draft.

Curran grew up in Snellville, but he always had thoughts of another place his family called home. Curran's family came to the United States from Liberia in the 1980s so that his mother could pursue a master's degree at Emory University. When civil war erupted in 1989, they had no option but to remain in Georgia.

Thus, throughout his childhood Rennie was influenced by his family's other home. "Growing up in my house was like growing up as close to Liberia as you can without actually being there," he said. "We'd eat the same food. My church was mostly people from Liberia, too." Since many family members remained in the war-torn country, Rennie's parents did what they could to support those back home. "We had family come and stay with us pretty often," Rennie recalled.

BULLDOGS

Even as he grew up and went to Athens, he knew his family's home only indirectly. "We never had the money to go back," he said, until the Tennessee Titans drafted him in 2010. With resources at his disposal, Curran fulfilled his "Liberian Dream." For ten days in April 2011 -- after 22 years -- Curran went home.

Getting that college degree. Running a marathon. Returning to the land of your birth. Getting married. Starting a new career. Though we may make all kinds of excuses, it's often never too late for life-changing decisions and milestones.

This is especially true in our faith life, which is based on God's promises through Jesus Christ. He showed up in Bethany four days late, as Martha pointed out, having seemingly dawdled a little as though the death of his friend Lazarus really didn't matter to him. It clearly did since he broke down and cried when he saw Lazarus' burial site. Being Jesus, however, he wasn't late; he was right on time because with Jesus there are no impossible situations or circumstances.

This is true in our own lives no matter how hopeless our current circumstances may appear to us. At any time – today even -- we can regret the things we have done wrong and the way we have lived, ask God in Jesus' name to forgive us, and discover a new way of living – forever.

With Jesus, it's never too late. He is always right on time.

That was my dream -- to go out there and meet the family I had never met before.
                              -- Rennie Curran on going home to Liberia

**It's never too late to change a life
by turning it over to Jesus.**

DEAD WRONG

Read Matthew 26:14-16; 27:1-10.

"When Judas, who had betrayed him, saw that Jesus was condemned, he was seized with remorse" (v. 27:3).

Some Florida coaches wound up being wrong -- even though they were right. As a result, the Bulldogs landed an All-American football player.

Herb St. John is the only UGA football player to be named All-SEC four times. From 1944-47, he was a starter on both sides of the UGA line. After the Dawgs went 11-0 in 1946 and were voted the national champions in one poll, he was named All-America.

St. John was raised in Jacksonville, Fla., and when the Gator head coach told him he had a scholarship for him, St. John said he would take it. The coach said he would get in touch with him later. "I figured I was going to Florida," St. John said.

Shortly thereafter, St. John received a Christmas card from the coach, but that was all he ever heard from Gainesville. Meanwhile, Mike Castronis, a former teammate of St. John's who was playing for Georgia at the time, came home for Christmas and told St. John the Bulldogs really wanted him up in Athens. Castronis was on his way to legendary Bulldog status himself as an All-American tackle in 1945.

St. John replied, "Tell them to send me a bus ticket, and I will come." The coaches did. "I got off the bus at 4:30 in the afternoon and by 5:00 I was registered in school," St. John recalled.

So what happened with the Gators? Only years later did St. John find out. While he was seeking a teacher's certificate, he took some courses at Florida, ran into a coach, and asked him why they never called him. It turned out the coaches had learned that St. John was about to be drafted, so they backed off.

They were right about that. In the middle of spring practice in 1945, St. John received his notice. Where the Gator coaching staff went wrong, though, was the physical. St. John flunked it and was sent back to Athens -- to become a Bulldog legend.

There's wrong, there's dead wrong, and there's Judas wrong. We've all been wrong in our lives, but we can at least honestly ease our conscience by telling ourselves we'll never be as wrong as Judas was. A close examination of Judas' actions, however, reveals that we can indeed replicate in our own lives the mistake Judas made that drove him to suicidal despair.

Judas ultimately regretted his betrayal of our Lord, but his sorrow and remorse, however boundless, could not save him. His attempt to undo his initial wrong was futile because he tried to fix everything himself rather than turning to God in repentance and begging for mercy.

While we can't literally betray Jesus to his enemies as Judas did, we can match Judas' failure in our own lives by not turning to God in Jesus' name and asking for forgiveness for our sins. In that case, we ultimately will be as dead wrong as Judas was.

I understand some of the Florida coaches caught [flak].
-- Herb St. John on Florida's mistake

A sin is the first wrong; failing to ask God for forgiveness of it is the second.

DAY 23

MEMORY LOSS

Read 1 Corinthians 11:17-29.

"[D]o this in remembrance of me" (v. 24).

Both his head coach and his quarterback told freshman running back Kregg Lumpkin to forget it and quit beating himself up. He did and scored the game-winning touchdown.

The Dogs of 2003 buried Clemson 30-0, South Carolina 31-7, Tennessee 41-14, Auburn 26-7, and Georgia Tech 34-17. They led Alabama 30-3 in the second quarter and coasted to a win. But they suffered a heartbreaking loss to LSU, yet another inexplicable meltdown in Jacksonville, and then a blowout loss to LSU in the league title game. At 10-3, they landed in the Capital One Bowl on New Year's Day to do battle with the 9-3 Purdue Boilermakers.

UGA jumped out to a 24-0 lead in the second quarter behind three scoring tosses from David Greene. Four years earlier in the 2000 Outback Bowl, the Dawgs had fallen behind Purdue 25-0 before rallying to win 28-25 in the greatest comeback in bowl history. On this day, however, with a little assist from Lumpkin, it was the Boilermakers' turn to put together an unbelievable rally.

A 3-yard touchdown pass with 1:41 left cut the UGA lead to 27-24. When the onside kick went out of bounds, the game was apparently over. But on second down, instead of just falling down when he was in trouble, Lumpkin reversed his field and had the ball punched out. Purdue recovered at the Bulldog 34 and kicked a field goal to tie the game with 49 seconds left. Overtime.

BULLDOGS

A disconsolate Lumpkin stood on the sideline, his head down. Head coach Mark Richt had some instructions for him. "Forget about it," Richt told him. "You need to get yourself ready to help us win this thing." Then he sent Lumpkin into the game.

On fourth and inches at the goal line, Lumpkin scored. When linebacker Tony Taylor nabbed an interception, the Dawgs had a 34-27 win they would not forget on a touchdown Kregg Lumpkin would always remember.

Memory makes us who we are. Whether our memories appear as pleasant reverie or unnerving nightmares, they shape us and to a large extent determine both our actions and our reactions. Alzheimer's is so terrifying because it steals our memory from us, and in the process we lose ourselves. We disappear.

The greatest tragedy of our lives is that God remembers. In response to that photographic memory, he condemns us for our sin. Paradoxically, the greatest joy of our lives is that God remembers. In response to that memory, he came as Jesus to wash even the memory of our sins away.

God uses memory as a tool through which we encounter revival. At the Last Supper, Jesus instructed his disciples and us to remember. In sharing this unique meal with fellow believers and remembering Jesus and his actions, we meet Christ again, not just as a memory, but as an actual living presence. To remember is to keep our faith alive.

Not in my huddle.
-- QB David Greene to Kregg Lumpkin, still replaying his fumble

**Because we remember Jesus,
God will not remember our sins.**

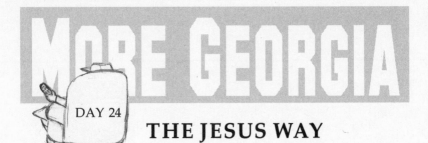

DAY 24

THE JESUS WAY

Read Romans 13:8-14.

"The night is nearly over; the day is almost here. So let us put aside the deeds of darkness and put on the armor of light" (v. 12).

From eating Fruit Loops to the way they smiled, the most celebrated twins in collegiate women's basketball history did things a certain way: the same way.

Twin sisters Coco and Kelly Miller shared the court at Georgia from 1997-2001. Coco was named to the All-SEC First Team in 1999 and 2001; she finished her career among the top ten in assists and steals for the Lady Dawgs. Kelly was named to the All-SEC First Team all four seasons and was the SEC Player of the Year in 2000 and '01. She was the first player in NCAA history to accumulate 1,500 points, 400 assists, and 200 steals.

Sports Illustrated described them as "a pair without peer, the most synchronized backcourt in NCAA history." That on-court synchronization was natural; they did everything the same way.

They wore similar clothes, had the same characteristic half-smile, and looked exactly alike "with the exception of a renegade freckle here and there." At team visits to IHOP, they both ordered buttermilk pancakes and drowned them in strawberry and blueberry syrup. "If one raises her fork, the other will too," observed teammate Camille Murphy. "I've seen them eat Fruit Loops," she said, "and without thinking about it, each of them leaves two

BULLDOGS

loops floating in her bowl. I'm like, Man!, how'd they do that?"

Dawg head coach Andy Landers admitted to fleeting moments of vertigo from watching them on the court. It wasn't just that they wore identical uniforms with identical white knee pads and identical brown ponytails. On the court, they often spoke to each other in a language only they could understand. Sometimes they even pulled off a play without any apparent communication at all.

In a last bit of inexplicable Miller togetherness, their pro careers ended when their two teams independently released them -- on the same day. Coco and Kelly Miller just do things the same way.

Like the Miller twins, you have a way of life that defines and describes you. You're a die-hard Bulldog fan for starters. Maybe you're married with a family. A city guy or a small-town gal. You wear jeans or a suit to work every day. And then there's your faith.

For the Christian, following Jesus more than anything else defines for the world your way of life. It's basically simple in its concept even if it is downright daunting in its execution. You act toward others in a way that would not embarrass you were your day to be broadcast on the national news. You think about others in a way that would not humiliate you should your thoughts be the plotline for a new reality show.

You make your actions and thoughts those of love: at all times, in all things, toward all people. It's the Jesus way of life, and it's the way to life forever with God.

At times Kelly and Coco seem to be halves of a single personality.
—SI's Franz Lidz on the Miller twins

To live the Jesus way is to act with love at all times, in all things, and toward all people.

LOST AND FOUND

Read Luke 15:11-32.

"This brother of yours was dead and is alive again; he was lost and is found" (v. 32).

He was "just another washed-up football player shooting pick-up hoops at a Southern California gym." He had lost forever the game he loved because of an injury. Or -- maybe not.

That player who wasn't playing was Jarvis Jones. As a freshman linebacker at Southern Cal in 2009, he suffered a spinal injury while making a tackle. The first doctor told Jones he would be fine and could play again. The Trojan team doctors, however, refused to clear him to play. They recommended he quit football.

So there he was, 20 years old and so desperate for sports that he considered trying out for the Trojan basketball team. All the while, though, Jones remembered that first doctor's favorable prognosis, and he wondered if other team doctors would clear him to play. He got his high-school coach to contact Georgia, Alabama, and FSU. To no one's surprise, the coaches said they wanted him if doctors gave him a clean bill of health.

UGA head coach Mark Richt was by Jones' side when he underwent tests at an Athens hospital. In their conversation, Jones told Richt that he missed sweet tea. "I knew we had a good chance," the head Dawg said. When the doctors cleared Jones to play, the two went to lunch. Over that meal in June 2010, Jones found his game again. "Coach, I'm a Dawg," he said.

BULLDOGS

After a redshirt year, Jones became a Bulldog legend. He started right away and capped his two seasons in Athens in the 45-31 win over Nebraska in the 2013 Capital One Bowl by breaking David Pollack's school record for sacks in a season. His 14.5 sacks led the nation. He declared for the NFL draft after the game, finishing his Bulldog career as a two-time All-America.

Jarvis Jones truly found that which he thought he had lost.

From car keys to friendships, fortunes to reading glasses, loss is a feature of the unfolding panorama of our lives. We win some, we lose some; that's life.

Loss may range from the devastatingly tragic to the momentarily annoying. No loss, however, is as permanently catastrophic as the loss of our very souls. While "being lost" is one of Christianity's many complex symbols, the concept is simple. The lost are those who have chosen to separate themselves from God, to live without an awareness of God in an unrepentant lifestyle contrary to his commandments and tenets. Being lost is a state of mind as much as a way of life.

It's a one-sided decision, though, since God never leaves the lost; they leave him. In God's eyes, no one is a born loser, and neither does anyone have to remain lost. All it takes is a turning back to God; all it takes is a falling into the open arms of Jesus Christ, the good shepherd.

I understand you never know when it's all going to be taken away.
-- Jarvis Jones on the time when he had lost football

From God's point of view, we are all either lost or found; interestingly, we – not God – determine into which group we land.

DAY 26

MAKE NO MISTAKE

Read Mark 14:66-72.

"Then Peter remembered the word Jesus had spoken to him: 'Before the rooster crows twice you will disown me three times.' And he broke down and wept" (v. 72).

The Bulldogs landed Bill Krug because the Maryland coaches made a mistake: They called him on the phone.

Krug was a first-team All-SEC defensive back in 1976 and '77. He helped make up the play that stopped Florida on "Fourth-and-Dumb." In Jacksonville in 1976, Florida led 27-20 and faced 4th-and-1 at its own 29 in the third quarter when the Gator coaches made a big mistake; they decided to go for it. On the play, end Dicky Clark's responsibility was the quarterback, but Krug told Clark to take the dive back and he would take the quarterback. That left cornerback Johnny Henderson alone on the pitch man. "Johnny, you're all by yourself," Krug told him.

As Krug put it, "It worked perfectly." Clark forced the Gator quarterback to pitch too early, and Henderson nailed the back for a loss. "The game was over," Krug said. "Florida was still ahead, but at that moment they knew they were beat." Krug was right. On their way to the SEC title, the Dawgs won 41-27.

Krug wasn't a lock to play for Georgia. He lived in Maryland, didn't know much about UGA, and was pretty much committed to the Terrapins. But one of Joe Tereshinski, Sr.'s boys, (See Devotion No. 50.) played against Krug, and Senior got the Dogs interested.

They were way behind, though. "Maryland pushed all the right buttons" was the way Krug described the recruiting.

When he made a visit to Athens, however, Krug liked what he saw. He told coaches from both schools that he wanted a week to think about it and not to call him. That's where the Terp coaches blew it; a few days later, they called. For Krug, that mistake made up his mind.

It's distressing but it's true: Like football coaches and Simon Peter, we all make mistakes. Only one perfect man ever walked on this earth, and no one of us is he. Some mistakes are just dumb. Like locking yourself out of your car or falling into a swimming pool with your clothes on.

Other mistakes are more significant and carry with them the potential for devastation. Like heading down a path to addiction. Committing a crime. Walking out on a spouse and the children.

All these mistakes, however, from the momentarily annoying to the life-altering tragic, share one aspect: They can all be forgiven in Christ. Other folks may not forgive us; we may not even forgive ourselves. But God will forgive us when we call upon him in Jesus' name.

Thus, the twofold fatal mistake we can make is ignoring the fact that we will die one day and subsequently ignoring the fact that Jesus is the only way to shun Hell and enter Heaven. We absolutely must get this one right.

I was leaning toward Georgia, but that [phone call] sealed the deal.
-- Bill Krug

Only one mistake we make sends us to Hell
when we die: ignoring Jesus while we live.

DAY 27

GOOD JOB

Read Matthew 25:14-30.

"His master replied, 'Well done, good and faithful servant!'" (v. 21)

Zippy Morocco did such a good job against Tennessee that the Volunteer head coach wrote him a letter praising his play.

From Youngstown, Ohio, Morocco came South in 1948 after accepting a football scholarship from Wally Butts. Life had not been so good for his family; he eagerly accepted the offer because it promised three meals a day and a roof over his head.

Morocco's first love was basketball, but UGA didn't offer any scholarships in those days, so he played both sports. He turned down an offer from the Philadelphia Eagles to use a fifth year of eligibility and play basketball for Georgia in 1952-53.

Without football limiting his practices, Morocco became a star and Georgia's first basketball All-America. He scored 590 points, which set a new SEC season scoring record, and was named the league's MVP. Dominique Wilkins in 1981 and Kentavious Cald-well-Pope in 2013 are the only other Bulldog players to win the award (now called the Player of the Year).

On Feb. 25, 1953, Morocco had the greatest night of his career. Against Tennessee, he poured in 38 points, a Bulldog record at the time. (Ronnie Hogue's 46 points against LSU in 1971 is now the record.) Trailing by one, Georgia held the ball for the last shot and flipped the ball to Morocco with five seconds left. He "knocked

BULLDOGS

the bottom out of the basket" to pull out the 87-86 upset.

Perhaps the most amazing aspect of Morocco's feat was the manner in which he scored. He used a two-handed set shot, and many of his points that night -- including that last-second winner -- came from 40 feet or so away from the basket.

The next day, Tennessee's head coach, Emmett Lowery, wrote Morocco a letter telling him how impressed he was with his play. "I don't believe I have ever seen a finer individual performance than you put on here last night," the coach wrote.

Good job. Well done. Way to go.

Those words make us all swell up a little like a puffer fish and smile no matter how hard we try not to. We may deny it in an honest attempt to be at least reasonably humble, but we all cherish praise. We work hard and we may be well rewarded for it financially, but a cold, hard paycheck is not always enough. We like to be told we're doing something well; we desire to be appreciated.

Nowhere, however, is that affirmation more important than when it comes from God himself. We will all meet God one day, which is intimidating even to consider. How our soul will ring with unspeakable joy on that day of days if we hear God's thundering voice say to us, "Well done, good and faithful servant."

Could anything else really matter other than doing a good job for God?

Although we hated losing the ball game last night, the team and myself, [and] the fans of Knoxville, all admired your outstanding performance.
-- UT head coach Emmett Lowery to Zippy Morocco

If we don't do a good job for God in our lives,
all our work elsewhere amounts to nothing.

DAY 28

IN THE KNOW

Read John 4:19-26, 39-42.

*"They said to the woman, . . . 'Now we have heard for
ourselves, and we know that this man really is the Savior
of the world'" (v. 42).*

Arriving in Athens, Bill Lewis had no idea how well the Georgia players knew the defense they were playing.

Lewis joined Vince Dooley's staff as the secondary coach upon Jim Pyburn's retirement. After Lewis' initial season, Dooley promoted him to defensive coordinator, a position he held until he took the head coaching job at East Carolina in 1989.

When Dooley made the offer on New Year's morning, Lewis said yes and immediately set out for Athens rather than attend a national coaches convention. As Dooley recalled it, the new coach hadn't been in his motel room fifteen minutes before he got a call from offensive coordinator Bill Pace telling Lewis he was leaving Georgia to take a position at Tennessee. This concerned the boss Dawg because his close relationship with Pace was one reason Lewis came on board. Pace smoothed over the situation, though, when he visited Lewis and reassured him that he wasn't leaving because of any problems with the Georgia program.

When the Bulldog staff returned to Athens from the convention, Lewis was waiting for his boss, defensive coordinator Erk Russell. "I asked for a copy of his defensive playbook," Lewis recalled, but Russell surprised him by replying that he didn't have a playbook.

BULLDOGS

"It's all up here," he said, tapping his bald head.

After that disconcerting introduction to the legendary Bulldog, Lewis and Russell sat down for a lengthy review. Lewis had yet another surprise waiting for him when he met his players. "It was amazing how well those players knew . . . that defense," he said.

Lewis went on to say that during his first season the players knew more about the Split 60 defense that he did. "I truly mean that," he said. "They coached me up on it."

No matter who knew what, it worked. This was 1980 -- and Dawgs the world over know what happened that season.

Lewis, Russell, and their Dawgs just knew that defense in the same way you know certain things in your life. That your spouse loves you, for instance. That you are good at your job. That tea should be iced and sweetened. That a bad day fishing is still better than a good day at work. You know these things even though no mathematician or philosopher can prove any of this on paper.

It's the same way with faith in Jesus: You just know that he is God's son and the savior of the world. You know it in the same way that you know Georgia is the only team worth pulling for: with every fiber of your being, with all your heart, your mind, and your soul. You know it despite the mindless babble and blasphemy of the unbelievers.

You just know, and because you know him, Jesus knows you. And that is all you really need to know.

Bill Lewis knew what all 22 guys were doing on every play.
-- Defensive back Bob Kelly, who nicknamed Lewis 'Mad Dog'

A life of faith is lived in certainty and conviction:
You just know you know.

DAY 29

PRAYER WARRIORS

Read Luke 18:1-8.

"Then Jesus told his disciples a parable to show them that they should always pray and not give up" (v. 1).

Prayers he didn't even know about changed Alec Millen's life.

Millen played two seasons on the offensive line at North Carolina before he tired of losing and transferred to Georgia. He had to sit out the 1990 season because of the transfer but was a starter at tackle in both '91 and '92.

Life was apparently pretty good for Millen in Athens. He was playing the game he loved; he had friends; he had received a good deal of positive publicity even before he played a down for the Dogs (He was, in fact, on his way to being named a third-team All-America by the Associated Press in 1992.); he had parties and he had girls. But something was wrong, although Millen didn't know exactly what. He just knew he felt an emptiness inside.

He had been raised in a Christian home, and he continued to attend an Athens church. His faith, however, was pretty much limited to one hour a week in that building. It was an empty faith.

Millen was unaware that all the while a teammate was praying for him. That anonymous Bulldog had been challenged by the team chaplain to make a list of people that he thought were "least likely" to be saved and to pray for them. That list included Alec Millen. For more than a year, beginning soon after Millen arrived in Athens, that player prayed for him daily. He also witnessed to the big lineman about Jesus, but met only rejection.

Finally, in May of 1991, Millen went along with others to a mid-week revival service at which a man testified about his faith in Jesus. Millen had never heard such a personal message, and God broke him on the spot. He was saved that night.

Millen eventually went to seminary and into the foreign mission field with his wife. He gave his life completely to Christ, and it all began with prayers he didn't even know were being lifted up for him.

Jesus taught us to do what that teammate of Alec Millen's did: always pray and never give up even if we don't see results right away. All too often we pray for a while about something – perhaps fervently at first – but our enthusiasm wanes if we don't receive the answer we want exactly when we want it. Why waste our time by asking for the same thing over and over again?

But God isn't deaf; God does hear our prayers, and God does respond to them. As Jesus clearly taught, our prayers have an impact because they turn the power of Almighty God loose in this world. Thus, falling to our knees and praying to God is not a sign of weakness and helplessness. Rather, praying for someone or something is an aggressive act, an intentional ministry, a conscious and fervent attempt on our part to change someone's life or the world for the better.

God responds to our prayers; we often just can't perceive or don't understand how he is working to answer those prayers.

God, if I can know you like this man knows you, I will do anything.
-- Alec Millen's prayer the night he was saved

Jesus taught us to always pray and never give up.

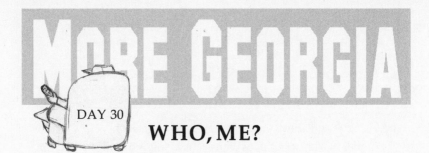

DAY 30

WHO, ME?

Read Judges 6:11-23.

"'But Lord,' Gideon asked, 'how can I save Israel? My clan is the weakest in Manasseh, and I am the least in my family'" (v. 15).

George Patton couldn't believe it when Vince Dooley told him to go in at quarterback, but he sure liked it. The opposition didn't believe it either, but they didn't like it one bit.

"The first dominant player of the Vince Dooley era," Patton was an All-American defensive tackle in 1965 and '66 and was All-SEC three times (1964-66). In high school, he was "a slow quarterback with a strong arm, who could throw it a long way." As Patton put it, "There weren't a whole lot of teams looking for a quarterback with no foot speed." In the fall of 1962, therefore, he was listed as the No. 6 quarterback on the Dawg depth chart. After a season on the freshman team, he was redshirted in 1963. "I didn't know if I was ever going to get on the field," he said.

But the new head coach started moving players around to get the best athletes on the field. When Dooley asked Patton if he would like to give defensive tackle a try, he didn't hesitate. With what speed he had and his experience at quarterback that let him anticipate plays, he was a natural.

His senior season the Dawgs won the SEC and stomped SMU 24-9 in the Cotton Bowl. After the last UGA defensive series in the bowl, Dooley surprised Patton by telling him to play quarterback.

When Patton informed the huddle what was going on, "Everybody just smiled." He told his receivers "to run as far and as fast as they could and I was going to throw it." He did just that, sailing three long incomplete passes.

The SMU players evidently figured Georgia was making fun of them by putting a tackle in at quarterback. When Patton ran the ball on fourth down, some of the Mustangs jumped on him and pummeled him with their fists. At a banquet that evening, Patton soothed everything over by telling the SMU team that his playing quarterback was to honor him and not to ridicule them.

Like George Patton against SMU, you've had your "Who, Me?" moments, though perhaps they haven't been as welcome as his was. Like the time you hadn't done your homework and -- sure enough -- the teacher called on you. Or the night the hypnotist picked you to be his guinea pig. You've known the turmoil in your midsection when you suddenly found yourself in a situation you neither sought nor were prepared for.

You may feel exactly as Gideon did about being called to serve God in some way, quailing at the very notion of being audacious enough to teach Sunday school, coordinate a high school prayer club, or lead a small group study. Who, me? Hey, who *is* worthy enough to do anything like that?

The truth is that nobody is – but that doesn't seem to matter to God. And it's his opinion, not yours, that counts.

I thought he was kidding.
    -- George Patton on Vince Dooley's telling him to play quarterback

You're right in that no one is worthy to serve God, but the problem is that doesn't matter to God.

DAY 31

RECIPE FOR DISASTER

Read Luke 21:5-11, 25-28.

"There will be great earthquakes, famines and pestilences in various places, and fearful events and great signs from heaven" (v. 11).

On a night when the Dawgs flirted with disaster -- none more so than their special teams -- it was a heads-up play on special teams that averted total disaster.

The Bulldogs were four-touchdown favorites on Oct. 20, 2012, against a Kentucky team that would win only two games, none in the SEC, and would fire its head coach. The Dawgs managed a 29-24 win, thereby barely avoiding a really disastrous loss.

Some things went right. Junior quarterback Aaron Murray threw for four touchdowns and for what was then a career-high 417 yards. He set a Georgia career record for touchdown passes. But, as Murray pointed out, "It got a little scary at points."

In fact, it was scary for most of the night, thanks partly to the special teams' ongoing flirtation with disaster. With UGA behind 14-7 in the second quarter, Murray hit Tavarres King for a 48-yard touchdown. The PAT was missed and Georgia still trailed. "The extra points shouldn't be that way," head coach Mark Richt said in a bit of wry understatement.

The special teams guys then had a chip-shot field goal for the lead right before halftime. Freshman Marshall Morgan promptly slammed his kick off the left upright before it wobbled through the goalposts. "I think (Morgan) has hit the uprights more than anybody in the nation," Richt said. "That one had to be in just by a fraction. I saw the official, and I don't know if he was sure."

Georgia led 29-17 before UK scored late and set up for the on-side kick. The Wildcat kicker executed it perfectly, and for a brief moment, the Dawgs flirted with disaster again. But junior walk-on Connor Norman dived into a wall of Kentucky players to claim the ball. Disaster averted, the Bulldogs ran out the clock.

We live in a world that seems to be either struck by one disaster after another or is the home of several ongoing and seemingly permanent disasters, all of them much more serious than losing a football game. Earthquakes virtually obliterate an entire nation; volcanoes erupt. Floods devastate cities and shatter lives; oil spills pollute our oceans and seashores. Can we even count the number of wars that are going on at any one time?

This apparently unending litany of disaster is enough to make us all give up hope. Maybe – but not for the followers of Jesus Christ. The truth is that Jesus' disciples should find reassurance of their ultimate hope in the world's constant disasters because this is exactly what Jesus said would happen.

These disasters indicate that the time of our redemption is drawing near. How near is up to God to decide. Nevertheless, this is a season of hope and great promise for those of the faith.

I think against Florida we'll play a lot better.
-- Linebacker Jordan Jenkins after the Kentucky game

**Jesus told us what to do when disaster
threatens to overwhelm us and our world:
'Stand up and lift up your heads.'**

DAY 32

WATER POWER

Read Acts 10:34-48.

"Can anyone keep these people from being baptized with water? They have received the Holy Spirit just as we have" (v. 47).

One of Georgia's more memorable wins on the gridiron is perhaps best remembered for what happened *after* the game, when some enthusiastic Bulldog fans had the water turned on them.

On Nov. 15, 1986, the 6-3 Dawgs took on 8th-ranked and 11-point favorite Auburn in The Loveliest Village. As if UGA didn't have problems enough, starting quarterback James Jackson failed to return from his grandmother's funeral. Backup Wayne Johnson got the start against one of the nation's toughest defenses.

Without Jackson, the Dawgs turned to their running game and ground out 239 tough yards. Lars Tate led the way with 94 yards with Keith Henderson adding 62 yards and fullback David Mc-Cluskey another 45. Johnson threw the ball sparingly, but he was effective, hitting six of seven passes including an 8-yard TD toss to tight end Troy Sadowski. He also rushed for a touchdown as UGA shocked the Tigers by taking a 20-10 lead late in the game.

But Auburn rallied in a desperate attempt to save itself. The Tigers drove 99 yards for a score with 2:51 on the clock. The Tiger defense then forced a Bulldog punt, and the offense roared down the field to the UGA 33 as the clock ticked under a minute. With 54 seconds left, linebacker Steve Boswell intercepted a pass to clinch the big upset.

The Dawg victory was as unexpected as what happened next. Exuberant Bulldog fans by the scores rushed onto the field and began tearing up turf for souvenirs. When they began pulling down the goalposts, Auburn security personnel responded by "spraying the enthusiasts with water cannons, including innocent Georgia bystanders."

The contest was subsequently dubbed "The Game Between the Hoses."

Children's wading pools and swimming pools in the backyard. Fishing, boating, skiing, and swimming at a lake. Sun, sand, and surf at the beach. If there's any water around, we'll probably be in it, on it, or near it. If there's not any at hand, we'll build a dam and create our own. Or turn on the water cannons.

We love the wet stuff for its recreational uses, but water first and foremost is about its absolute necessity to support and maintain life. From its earliest days, the Christian church appropriated water as an image of life through the ritual of baptism. Since the time of the arrival of the Holy Spirit at Pentecost, baptism with water has been the symbol of entry into the Christian community. It is water that marks a person as belonging to Jesus. It is through water that a person proclaims that Jesus is his Lord.

There's something in the water, all right. There is life.

It was the first time Jordan-Hare Stadium used its water cannons for crowd control.

– Vince Dooley on the '86 Auburn game

There is life in the water:
physical life and spiritual life.

DAY 33

GOOD NEWS

Read Matthew 28:1-10.

'"He has risen from the dead and is going ahead of you into Galilee. There you will see him.' Now I have told you" (v. 7).

Ty Frix twice got some really good news while he was a Georgia football player. In both instances, he was clueless about what was to happen.

Frix walked on to the team in 2008. After a redshirt season, he handled all the snapping duties for the Dawgs from 2009-2012, starting 54 straight games. He thus followed in the footsteps of his dad, Mitch Frix, who was Georgia's snapper in 1981 and '82.

As a walk-on, Frix was handed a jersey that lacked what he called a "real number." He started out at no. 132 and moved up (or down) to no. 112. Before the 2009 season, placekicker Blair Walsh called his snapper and said he had something to tell him. "What's up?" Frix asked, but Walsh told him he would have to wait and see. "Come to the locker room because we need to kick."

In the locker room, a bewildered Frix couldn't find his locker until an amused Walsh pointed something out. Frix had been moved "into the real locker room and I had a real number."

In the spring of 2010, Frix returned home and crawled back into bed after an 8 a.m. final. (The biological engineering major was accepted into medical school in 2013.) He got a phone call from an "unknown number," so he put the phone down and went back to sleep. When it rang again, he figured he'd better answer it. It was head coach Mark Richt, who told Frix to be in his office Monday morning. Figuring he was in real trouble, Frix immediately called his dad. "We were so worried about it," he recalled. The senior Frix even drove down from Calhoun and waited while his son was in Richt's office.

When Ty walked out, though, he was beaming. Richt had just told him the good news that he had earned a scholarship.

The story of mankind's "progress" through the millennia could be summarized and illustrated quite well in an account of how we disseminate our news. For much of recorded history, we told our stories through word of mouth, which required time to spread across political and geographical boundaries. That method also didn't do much to ensure accuracy.

Today, though, our news – unlike that which Ty Frix received -- is usually instantaneous. Yesterday's news is old news; we want to see it and hear about it as it happens.

But the biggest news story in the history of the world goes virtually unnoticed every day by the so-called mainstream media. It is, in fact, often treated as nothing more than superstition. But it's true, and it is the greatest, most wonderful news of all.

What headline should be blaring from every news source in the world? This one: "Jesus Rises from Dead, Defeats Death." It's still today's news, and it's still the most important news story ever.

That was something you never even dream about.
-- Ty Frix on learning he had been given 'a real number'

The biggest news story in history took place when Jesus Christ walked out of that tomb.

A HEX ON YOU

Read Jonah 1.

"Tell us, who is responsible for making all this trouble for us? What did you do?" (v. 8a)

Y ou would think a coach would be right there cheering on one of his former players as he won his first pro tournament. Not UGA's Chris Haack. He stayed away to avoid jinxing former Bulldog All-American Hudson Swafford.

Since Haack was named the Bulldogs' men's golf coach in 1996, he has led the squad to two national titles, two runners-up spots, and seven SEC titles. He and assistant UGA coach Jim Douglas were among the interested spectators when Swafford, a rookie on the Nationwide Tour, teed off for the final around of the 2012 Stadion Classic at the UGA golf course. They watched apprehensively as Swafford bogeyed the first hole, and the superstitious Haack decided the coaches' presence was jinxing Swafford.

So he turned to Douglas and said, "I'll tell you what; let's just go distance ourselves." And so they did, trekking across the course to a pavilion near the 17th hole. There they waited, watching the leader board instead of Swafford.

After that shaky start, Swafford got hot. When he approached the tee at 17, he had birdied eight holes and had the lead. Even then, Haack and Douglas didn't watch him. "We were behind a part of the tent," Haack said. "We couldn't even see the green [at 17], and we didn't even get out of our chairs to watch him. We were staying right where we were because we're superstitious and didn't want to move."

When Swafford birdied both 17 and 18, the coaches knew from the roar of the crowd that something good had happened. Even after Swafford finished, setting a course record with a 62, the pair didn't move for fear of resurrecting the jinx. They waited on all the contenders to come in before they finally located their former star and the new Stadion champion to congratulate him.

Fear of hexes and jinxes and the like really does belong to the domain of superstitious nonsense, though Chris Haack may be difficult to convince after the 2012 Stadion Classic.

Some people do feel, however, that they exist under a dark and rainy cloud. Nothing goes right; all their dreams collapse around them; they seem to constantly bring about misery on themselves and also on the ones around them. Why? Is it really a hex, a jinx?

Nonsense. The Bible provides us an excellent example in Jonah. The sailors on the boat with Jonah believed him to be a hex and the source of their bad luck. Jonah's life was a mess, but it had nothing to do with any jinx. His life was in shambles because he was disobeying God.

Take a careful look at people you know whose lives are in shambles, including some who profess to believe in God. The key to life lies not in belief alone; the responsibility of the believer is to obey God. Problems lie not in hexes but in disobedience.

He knows us well enough to know we're very superstitious.
-- Chris Haack on jinxing Hudson Swafford

Hexes don't cause us trouble,
but disobedience to God sure does.

DAY 35

THE GREATEST

Read Mark 9:33-37.

"If anyone wants to be first, he must be the very last, and the servant of all" (v. 35).

Mike Bobo saved his greatest game for the last. The proof is right there in the NCAA record book.

As a senior in 1997, Bobo led Division 1-A in passing efficiency; his completion percentage that season (65.0) remains the Bulldog record. He led the Dogs to a 10-2 record and a win over Wisconsin in the 1998 Outback Bowl.

After his final game, Bobo served as a graduate assistant under Jim Donnan before moving to Jacksonville State as the quarterbacks coach. When Mark Richt set about assembling his first staff in 2001, he brought him back to Athens as quarterbacks coach before naming him offensive coordinator in 2007.

Bobo didn't have a very good week of practice leading up to the 1998 bowl game. "I don't think I threw one spiral all week," he said. "I hardly completed anything at practice. It was cold, it was damp and I threw the ball terrible." Then Bobo took the field against the Badgers and made bowl-game history. Georgia buried Wisconsin 33-6 with Bobo doing whatever he wanted to.

He had plenty of help. Hines Ward set an Outback-Bowl record with twelve receptions for 154 yards, and Robert Edwards set a Georgia bowl record with three rushing scores.

And then there was Bobo. He passed for 267 yards, which

wasn't that outstanding, seeing as how he drilled Georgia Tech for 415 yards in the season finale. In amassing those 267 yards, though, he completed 26 of 28 passes, an all-time bowl record passing percentage of .929. He also set the all-time bowl record with 19 straight completions.

Bobo's only misses were a drop and one he intentionally threw away under duress. "My last college pass was a touchdown," he recalled. "I had guys make plays. It was a good day."

No, it was the greatest day of his Bulldog career.

We all want to be the greatest. The goal for the Bulldogs and their fans every season is the national championship. The competition at work is to be the most productive sales person on the staff or the Teacher of the Year. In other words, we define being the greatest in terms of the struggle for personal success. It's nothing new; Jesus' disciples saw greatness in the same way.

As Jesus illustrated, though, greatness in the Kingdom of God has nothing to do with the secular world's understanding of success. Rather, the greatest are those who channel their ambition toward the furtherance of Christ's kingdom through love and service, rather than their own advancement, which is a complete reversal of status and values as the world sees them.

After all, who could be greater than the person who has Jesus for a brother and God for a father? And that's every one of us.

It was one of those days when I couldn't miss.
                                        -- Mike Bobo on the Outback Bowl

**To be great for God has nothing to do
with personal advancement and everything to do
with the advancement of Christ's kingdom.**

THE GREATEST   73

DAY 36

SMART MOVE

Read 1 Kings 4:29-34; 11:1-6.

"[Solomon] was wiser than any other man. . . . As Solomon grew old, his wives turned his heart after other gods, and his heart was not fully devoted to the Lord his God" (vv. 4:31, 11:4).

Mixon Robinson made a smart move in part because he didn't want to have to study all the time in college.

A senior in 1967, Robinson made recruiting visits with a high-school buddy and quickly narrowed his choices to Alabama, Duke, and Georgia. His first trip was to Alabama, and "Man, it was 100 percent football all the time," Robinson said. "I thought that might be a bit too much for me."

Then it was on to Duke, and he liked it. He had a brother at Harvard and a sister at Vanderbilt, and the academic challenges Duke presented appealed to him.

So Duke it was -- until he told his buddy. "You need to think real hard about that," was the response. He told Robinson he would never have any fun because he would be studying all the time. That gave Robinson pause, and so when UGA coaches Erk Russell and John Donaldson called, he decided to play for UGA. Several factors in addition to the academics played into Robinson's decision, including the presence of his girlfriend at Georgia and the fact that his dad was a big Dawg fan.

Robinson was a backup tight end as a sophomore in 1969. In

the spring of 1970, Russell moved him to defensive end. In 1971, he was All-SEC as the Dawgs went 11-1.

About those academics. Robinson was in reality a quite serious student who went on to medical school and a career in Athens as an orthopedic surgeon. So he was All-SEC, married his wife, got into medical school, and spent his career "around a university and a town I really love."

In deciding on UGA, Mixon Robinson made a smart move.

Remember that time you wrecked the car when you spilled hot coffee on your lap? That cold morning you fell out of the boat? The time you gave your honey a tool box for her birthday?

Formal education notwithstanding, we all make some dumb moves sometimes because time spent in a classroom is not an accurate gauge of common sense. Folks impressed with their own smarts often grace us with erudite pronouncements that we intuitively recognize as flawed, unworkable, or simply wrong.

A good example is the observation that great intelligence and scholarship are inherently incompatible with a deep and abiding faith in God. That is, the more we know, the less we believe. Any incompatibility occurs, however, only because we begin to trust in our own wisdom rather than the wisdom of God. We forget, as Solomon did, that God is the ultimate source of all our knowledge and wisdom and that even our ability to learn is a gift from God.

Not smart at all.

I knew I could get a good education at Georgia.
-- Mixon Robinson on his smart move to attend UGA

Being truly smart means trusting in God's
wisdom rather than only in our own knowledge.

DAY 37

ALL IN

Read Mark 12:28-34.

"Love the Lord your God with all your heart and with all your soul and with all your mind and with all your strength" (v. 30).

The Dawgs were so enthusiastic in the wake of their sudden win over Alabama that a 330-lb. lineman couldn't breathe.

On their way to a No.-2 final ranking, the Bulldogs of 2007 found themselves with an overtime game on their hands against the Tide in Tuscaloosa on Sept. 22. Alabama kicked a field goal on its first possession for a 23-20 lead.

Calling plays for the first time, offensive coordinator Mike Bobo pondered his options and decided to try to win the game on the first play. With the pass designed to go deep into the corner, the play was a relatively safe one. The Dawgs could always kick a field goal if the offense couldn't recover from a first-down incompletion. And all night long, Alabama's coverage on first down had been fairly consistent. The play was designed to exploit that.

So Bobo went for it. Sure enough, the Tide lined up just as he had expected. That meant senior wide receiver Mikey Henderson, who was so fast his high school coach had tabbed him 'Blur,' had a good chance to beat the cornerback off the line. A play fake by quarterback Matthew Stafford would freeze the safety, enabling Henderson to get free in the end zone. The play worked to perfection with Henderson making an over-the-shoulder catch in the corner. With one play, Georgia had a 26-23 win.

Like their fans, the players erupted in celebration -- except for Henderson. He had lost track of the score and thought Georgia still needed to kick the extra point to win. He was clued in when 330-lb. lineman Chester Adams, nicknamed "Cheese," flattened him with an old wrestling move to start a dogpile. The rest of the enthusiastic team soon followed suit, piling on Henderson and Adams. "I heard Cheese say that he couldn't breathe," Henderson recalled. "I knew that I must have been in trouble, too."

What fills your life, your heart, and your soul so much that you sometimes just can't help what you do? We all have zeal and enthusiasm for something, whether it's Bulldog football, sports cars, our family, scuba diving, or stamp collecting.

But do we have a zeal for the Lord? We may well jump up and down, scream, holler, even cry – generally making a spectacle of ourselves – when Georgia scores. Yet on Sunday morning, if we go to church at all, we probably sit there showing about as much enthusiasm as we would for a root canal.

Of all the divine rules, regulations, and commandments we find in the Bible, Jesus made it crystal clear which one is number one: We are to love God with everything we have. All our heart, all our soul, all our mind, all our strength.

If we do that, our zeal and enthusiasm will burst forth. Like the Dawgs after beating Bama, we just won't be able to help ourselves.

We got to kick the extra point!
-- Mikey Henderson to his exuberant teammates after his TD catch

The enthusiasm with which we worship God
reveals the depth of our relationship with him.

DAY 38

THE 'I' IN PRIDE

Read 1 John 2:15-17.

"Everything in the world -- the desire of the flesh, the desire of the eyes, the pride in riches -- comes not from the Father but from the world" (v. 16 NRSV).

Tavarres King was proud of his personal achievements while he wore the red and black, but as his playing days ended, he was especially proud that he helped bring the swagger back.

King could well be the best unpublicized wide receiver in Bulldog football history. He set a record that is a great trivia question: Who has played in more football games than anyone else in school history? It's King, 56 of them. He played in twelve games in 2009 and 2010 and fourteen in 2011 and 2012. What makes his record virtually unbreakable is that he also played in four games in 2008 before suffering an injury and receiving a medical redshirt. Four games is the maximum the NCAA allows for a medical redshirt.

King quietly put together a spectacular career in Athens. His 2,602 receiving yards are the fourth-most in school history behind Terrence Edwards, Fred Gibson, and A.J. Green. His 21 career touchdown catches are the third most, behind only Edwards (30) and Green (23).

King knew the bad times of the 6-7 season of 2010. "You can't get any lower than [that] season," he said. He also knew the heartbreak of the excruciating loss to Alabama in the 2012 SEC title game. "It was the toughest loss I've ever been a part of," he said.

BULLDOGS

"We expected to win."

But King also knew some good times. He is proud that in 2011 and 2012, the Dogs won 21 of 27 games and two SEC East titles. "I think my class and the class before mine changed the culture around here, got Georgia back to its winning ways," he said. "I feel like we've gotten that [swagger] back."

And Tavarres King is proud of that.

What are you most proud of? The size of your bank account? The trophies from your tennis league? The title under your name at the office? Your family?

Pride is one of life's great paradoxes. You certainly want a surgeon who takes pride in her work or a Bulldog coach who is proud of his team's accomplishments. But pride in the things and the people of this world is inevitably disappointing because it leads to dependence upon things that will pass away and idolization of people who will fail you. Self-pride is even more dangerous because it inevitably leads to self-glorification.

Pride in the world's baubles and its people lures you to the earthly and the temporary, and away from God and the eternal. Pride in yourself yields the same results in that you exalt yourself and not God.

God alone is glorious enough to be worshipped. Jesus Christ alone is Lord.

We're leaving behind a program that is headed in the right direction.
-- Tavarres King on what he is proud of

Pride can be dangerous because it tempts you to lower your sight from God and the eternal to the world and the temporary.

DAY 39

NO JOKE!

Read Romans 12:9-21.

"Do not be overcome by evil, but overcome evil with good"
(v. 21).

No joke. Vince Dooley, who coached some of the greatest and most famous athletes of his time, once said that the most incredible player he ever had was a walk-on who appeared in one game.

Mike Steele walked on to the Bulldog football team and stayed for five seasons, never missing a day of practice. During two-a-days, when other players struggled just to get back to the dorm, Steele drove home and worked on the farm with his father. He played a little in the 44-0 romp over Tennessee in 1981; that was it.

At practice, All-SEC defensive guard Eddie "Meat Cleaver" Weaver "used to try to kill [Steele]," said fellow guard Tim Crowe. Weaver would forearm Steele, and "there would be blood all over the place." The blood resulted from a screw in Steele's facemask that he refused to have cut off. "Blood makes me tough," he said.

Even as an ROTC student, Steele wanted to be in Special Forces. He loved rappelling and once was arrested by campus police for rappelling off the bridge at the stadium. "He was just innocently doing that," Dooley said. After he left Athens, Steele was a leader in the *Black Hawk Down* incident in Somalia. He received a Bronze Star for his valor.

He subsequently developed a staph infection, though, and was given up for dead, even receiving last rites. No joke: He pulled

BULLDOGS

himself out of the hospital bed, went down the hall, and climbed on a treadmill. The exercise drove the blood clots that had been killing him out of his lungs.

Though he didn't succeed on the turf of Sanford Stadium as a Bulldog football player, Mike Steele's time in Athens was no joke. Witness Vince Dooley's admiration of him and Crowe's declaration, "If there was ever going to be a hero, he is my hero."

Certainly the Bible is not a repository of side-splitting jokes, though some theologians have posited that Jesus' parables were actually sort of jokes for his time. Have you heard the one about the son who left his rich father and went to live with pigs?

No, the Gospel and its message of salvation and hope is serious stuff. Christians take it as such and well they should. Yet, though many Christians would vilify anyone who treats Jesus as a joke, those same persons themselves treat some aspects of Jesus' teachings as little more than gags not to be taken seriously.

Sexual purity, for instance. How outdated is that? And the idea of expecting answers to our prayers. What a silly notion! Surely Jesus was jesting when he spoke of tithing. How laughable is it to live performing selfless acts for others without getting the credit! And polls consistently reveal that about half of America's Christians don't believe in Hell. In other words, Jesus was joking.

No, he wasn't. If we think any of what Jesus taught us is a joke, then the joke's on us – and it's not very funny.

Here I am fixing to kick the bucket and I'm watching The Flintstones.
-- Mike Steele after receiving last rites in the hospital

Jesus wasn't joking; if we truly love him, then we will live in the manner he prescribed for us.

NO JOKE! 81

DAY 40

GOOD TIMES

Read Psalm 30.

*"You turned my wailing into dancing; you removed my
sackcloth and clothed me with joy" (v. 11).*

They didn't win much and the whole staff got canned, but for
Mark Fox and his wife the University of Washington conjures up
memories of some good times.

Fox became the men's head basketball coach at Georgia in April
2009 after five successful seasons as the head man at the University of Nevada. He also spent four seasons in Reno as an assistant
and six seasons on the staff at Kansas State.

Fox got his coaching start from 1991-93 as a graduate assistant
and then an assistant coach at the University of Washington. His
two seasons there weren't exactly good times for the program.
They won 12 and 13 games and went a dismal 12-24 in the Pac 10,
finishing eighth in the league both years.

"We were getting crushed," recalled Mark Pope, who played
when Fox was there and served for one season at UGA as opera-
tions coordinator. "We just weren't very good." The women's
team even outdrew the men at the time. Pope said, "They fired
coach, fired me, fired the whole lot of us and started from scratch."

So how did this lack of success on the court translate into
good times for the Fox family? Well, Mark launched a friendship
with an assistant coach who introduced him to Cindy Holt, who
worked in the Huskies' promotions department. The two started

dating. Since Holt made more money than Fox did, she frequently picked up the tab. Four years after they first met each other, they were married on a rare sunny day in May in Seattle.

On a radio show in 2011, Mark spoke of his "fond memories of some of my times at [Washington]." Cindy also remembers those days as good times with "so many great places to go that didn't cost a lot of money."

Quite a bit has changed for the Fox folks since then, especially financially, but the memories of those good times still remain.

Here's a basic but distressing fact about the good times in our lives: They don't last. We may laugh in the sunshine today, but we do so while we symbolically glance over a shoulder. The Dawgs pull off the upset today and then turn around and lose later. We know that sometime – maybe tomorrow – we will cry in the rain as the good times suddenly come crashing down around us.

Awareness of the certainty that good times don't endure often drives many of us to lose our lives and our souls in a lifestyle devoted to the frenetic pursuit of "fun." This is nothing more, though, than a frantic, pitiable, and doomed effort to outrun the bad times lurking around the corner.

The good times will come and go. Only when we quit chasing the good times and instead seek the good life through Jesus Christ do we discover an eternity in which the good times will never end. Only then will we be forever joyous.

It was a great time, just young people that loved what they were doing.
– Cindy Fox on those early days at Washington

Let the good times roll – forever and ever
for the followers of Jesus Christ.

DAY 41

FIREPROOF

Read Malachi 3:1-5.

"Who can endure the day of his coming? Who can stand when he appears? For he will be like a refiner's fire or a launderer's soap. He will sit as a refiner and purifier of silver" (vv. 2, 3a).

One of George Collins' most indelible memories is of the day the Bulldogs had Gator fans practicing for a fire.

Collins was an All-American guard and a team captain as a senior in 1977 and was a star on the offensive line for the '76 SEC champs. Injuries and academic casualties forced the coaches to move him to tight end as a sophomore. The first day he showed up for practice at his new position, tight end Richard Appleby and wide receiver Gene Washington stopped him before he made it to the field. They told him, "You can't look like an offensive lineman if you're going to play tight end!" So they showed Collins how to put tape on his shoes for a little flash and how to get open.

But Collins wasn't in the lineup to catch passes. "All I did was block," he recalled. He was a part of the legendary Appleby-to-Washington bomb that beat Florida 10-7 in 1975. The Gators were packing the line, and the coaches decided to put Collins in as the second tight end to give Appleby more time to throw the ball even though they had never practiced the play out of that formation.

Just as memorable for Collins as the play was what happened after Georgia got the ball back and set about running out the

BULLDOGS

clock. To the Bulldogs' immense delight, the Florida fans began streaming to the exits. "That's when I first heard the term 'Fire Drill,'" Collins said. "The Florida fans were leaving that stadium so fast that we called it a fire drill."

The vast majority of us never face the horror and agony of literal fire. For most of us, fire conjures up images of romantic evenings before a fireplace, fond memories of hot dogs, marshmallows, and ghost stories around a campfire, or rib eyes sizzling on a grill. Even a fire drill by Gator fans.

Yet we appreciate that fire also has the capacity to destroy. The Bible reflects fire's dual nature, using it to describe almighty God himself and as a metaphor for both punishment and purification. God appeared to Moses in a burning bush and led the wandering Israelites by night as a pillar of fire. Malachi describes Jesus as a purifying and refining fire.

Fire is also the ultimate symbol for the destructive force of God's wrath, a side to God we quite understandably prefer not to dwell upon. Our sin and disobedience, though, not only break God's heart but also anger him.

Thus, fire in the Bible is basically a symbol for God's holiness. Whether that holiness destroys us or purifies us is the choice we make in our response to Jesus. We are, all of us, tested by fire.

It was really great being in that huddle and watching all of those Gators pour out of that place.
-- George Collins on the Gator fire drill in '75

**The holy fire of God is either the total destroyer
or the ultimate purifier;
we are fireproof only in Jesus.**

DAY 42

FIRST IMPRESSION

Read John 1:1-18.

"In the beginning was the Word, and the Word was with God, and the Word was God. . . . The Word became flesh and made his dwelling among us" (vv. 1, 14).

Art DeCarlo didn't make much of a first impression on head Dawg Wally Butts. That all changed once he got into a game.

DeCarlo was out of Youngstown, Ohio, a Bulldog hotbed of the 1940s and 1950s that sent Frank Sinkwich, All-American end George Poschner, and All-SEC defensive back Al Bodine, among others, to Athens.

Orphaned at 14 and living with an older brother after graduation, DeCarlo faced the prospect of life in the steel mills until Bodine, who played for Butts from 1947-49, recommended him to his former coach. Still, what Butts saw was a player who stood 6-foot-3 but who weighed only 167 pounds, and he didn't particularly like it. But DeCarlo's high school coach convinced Butts to move beyond his first impression and offer him a scholarship.

As DeCarlo's son remembered it, Bodine "gave my dad a one-way ticket down to Georgia and said, 'good luck.'" DeCarlo left behind everything he knew to play for a coach who wasn't too impressed with him to begin with.

It didn't take DeCarlo long to change Butts' impression. In his first four games in Athens as a sophomore in 1950, he recovered an incredible eight fumbles. He was one of the most versatile players in UGA history, playing center, linebacker, offensive end, and defensive back. He was twice All-SEC and went on to a pro career that included playing for the Baltimore Colts in the legendary overtime championship game of 1958.

One writer said that had the Bulldog football team held a popularity contest in the early 1950s, "DeCarlo would have won by a landslide." Not a bad impression to leave behind.

That guy in the apartment next door. A job search complete with interview. A twenty-year class reunion. The new neighbors. We are constantly about the fraught task of wanting to make an impression on people, especially that first one. We want them to remember us, obviously in a flattering way.

We make that impression, good or bad, generally in two ways. Even with instant communication on the Internet – perhaps especially with the Internet – we primarily influence the opinion others have of us by our words. After that, we can advance to the next level by making an impression with our actions.

God gave us an impression of himself in the same way. In Jesus, God took the unprecedented step of appearing to mortals as one of us, as mere flesh and bone. We now know for all time the sorts of things God does and the sorts of things God says.

In Jesus, God put his divine foot forward to make a good impression on each one of us.

Art DeCarlo was one of the finest competitors ever to play for the Red and Black.
    -- Wally Butts, changing his first impression of Art DeCarlo

**Through Jesus' words and actions,
God seeks to impress us with his love.**

DAY 43

BONE TIRED

Read Matthew 11:27-30.

"Come to me, all you who are weary and burdened, and I will give you rest" (v. 11).

Mark Richt was tired to the bone, but he couldn't let the Georgia people down.

When the glorious season of 2002 with its SEC championship ended, Richt didn't get any down time. Instead, the pace of the head coach's life actually picked up. What he called "the grind" was insane as the entire Bulldog Nation celebrated and wanted their coach to join them at the party.

Richt's basic problem was that he loved the Georgia people for their enthusiasm, their passion, and their love for his team. In the off-season that was the winter of 2003, "the SEC Coach of the Year was the property of his people." And it wore him down.

One evening he spoke to a Snellville church, his third public function that day. "As the echo died on the 'Amen' of his closing prayer, he realized just how bone tired he was." The head Dawg decided he could forgo the hour-long autograph session that capped all his speeches. He made his escape to the parking lot.

At a traffic light, Richt spotted a little boy with a ball cap seeking a signature. He rolled down the window, signed the cap, and told his driver to turn around. It didn't matter how tired he was; at the church, he would write his name as many times as the people wanted. He "rebuked himself for the un-Dawglike crime of failing to finish the drill with his fans."

When Richt arrived, though, people were on their way home. He had returned too late to make amends. That didn't matter; this had to be made right. The weary head coach and his assistant arranged with the "surprised and delighted congregation" for him to return the next day for an extended autograph session.

As they do sometimes with Mark Richt, the everyday struggles and burdens of life often beat us down. They may be enormous; they may be trivial with a cumulative effect. But they wear us out, so much so that we've even come up with a name for our exhaustion: chronic fatigue syndrome.

Doctors don't help too much. Sleeping pills can zonk us out; muscle relaxers can dull the weariness. Other than that, it's drag on as best we can until we can collapse exhaustedly into bed.

Then along comes Jesus, as usual offering hope and relief for what ails us, though in a totally unexpected way. He says take my yoke. Whoa, there! Isn't a yoke a device for work? Exactly.

The mistake we all too often make lies in trying to do it alone. We rely on ourselves instead of Jesus. If we yoke ourselves to our Lord, the unimaginable, limitless power of almighty God is at our disposal to do the heavy lifting for us..

God's strong shoulders and broad back can handle any burdens we can give him. We just have to let them go.

The 'no-huddle' lifestyle had caught up with him.
-- Writer Rob Suggs on Mark Richt in Snellville

**Tired and weary are a way of life
only when we fail to accept Jesus' invitation
to swap our burden for his.**

DAY 44

ONE-MAN ARMY

Read Revelation 19:11-21.

"The rest of them were killed by the sword that came out of the mouth of the rider on the horse" (v. 21).

Outlined against a backdrop of gray skies and turbulent winds off the St. John's River, . . . the one horseman rode again." So did Loran Smith poetically describe the one-man wrecking crew that was junior linebacker Jarvis Jones in the 2012 Florida game.

For Bulldog fans, the 17-9 win over the third-ranked Gators was an instant classic. Not only did the game propel the Dawgs into the SEC championship game and within a handful of yards of a shot at the national title, but it wrecked the Gators' league and national championship hopes. Perhaps not since 1980 has a victory over Florida been so delicious.

And right in the middle of it all was Jones, who, Smith asserted, played a game that matched the best outing of Bulldog legends Jake Scott, David Pollack, Terry Hoage, and Bill Stanfill. Jones' game stats support such high praise: thirteen tackles, including twelve solos and 4.5 for loss, three sacks, two forced fumbles, and two fumbles recovered. And this was not against a lesser opponent but in UGA's biggest game in years against the best Gator team in years.

Jones used his remarkable instincts to wreak havoc on the Florida offense, but he was free to do so because of the Bulldogs around him. The emergence of freshman linebacker Jordan Jenkins and the improved play of junior end Garrison Smith meant defensive coordinator Todd Grantham was able, as he put it, to "formation" Jones, moving him about before the snap. "We were lining him up where the ball was," Grantham joked.

But that's exactly where Jones consistently wound up, a one-man army who "played like he was lined up in the Gator backfield."

A similar situation will occur when Christ returns. He will not come back to us as the meek lamb led unprotestingly to slaughter on the cross. Instead, he will be a one-man army, a rider on a white horse who will destroy those forces responsible for disorder and chaos in God's world.

This image of our Jesus as a warrior may quite appropriately shock and discomfort us, but it should also excite and thrill us. It reminds us vividly that God will unleash his awesome power to effect justice and righteousness in a world that persecutes his people and slanders his name. It should also lend us a sense of urgency because the time will pass when decisions for Christ can still be made.

For now, Jesus has an army at his disposal in the billions of Christians around the world. We are Christian soldiers; we have a world to conquer for our Lord – before he returns as a one-man army to finish the job.

[In] Bulldog history, there has not been a one-man defensive performance comparable to the one [Jarvis Jones] put on at EverBank Field.
-- Loran Smith on Jones' play vs. Florida in 2012

Jesus will return as a one-man army to conquer the forces of evil; for now, we are his army.

DAY 45

GREAT EXPECTATIONS

Read John 1:43-51.

"'Nazareth! Can anything good come from there?'
Nathanael asked" (v. 46).

The Bulldog faithful were pretty consistent about their expectations for the new head football coach. They weren't met.

As the 1963 football season ended, "Georgia was in a desperate situation." Seven of the last nine teams had had losing records. The athletic department was struggling financially and with its fan base. In perhaps the ultimate humiliation, UGA played Miss. State at Georgia Tech's Grant Field in an effort to boost attendance.

New Athletic Director Joel Eaves' first job was to hire a new coach. The expectations were clear: He had to be a "name" coach, a proven winner who would excite and unite the fan base.

What they got was an assistant coach who was so unknown that university president O.C. Aderhold forgot his name at the press conference announcing his hiring. The athletic board was described as shocked and downcast at the hiring of a 31-year-old they had never heard of who had no head coaching experience.

The new coach's first game was against Alabama. On the first play, future All-American tackle George Patton dropped the Tide runner for a loss. Radio color man Bill Munday screamed into his microphone, "Gawja's ready! Gawja's ready!" So were Alabama and Joe Namath; the Tide cruised to a 31-3 win. "As the conventional wisdom went the next week, 'What did you expect?'"

BULLDOGS

Whatever the expectations were, Vince Dooley exceeded them. What Georgia got was a revered coach who won 201 games, six SEC titles, and one national championship. He was the national coach of the year twice and the SEC coach of the year seven times. In 1994, he was inducted into the College Football Hall of Fame.

Over the course of his 40-year association with the university as coach and athletic director, Dooley led UGA into the modern era of college sports, cementing the school's place as an athletic powerhouse where great expectations are the norm every year.

The blind date your friend promised would look like Brad Pitt or Jennifer Aniston but resembled a Munster or Cousin Itt. Your vacation that went downhill after the lost luggage. Quite often in life, your expectations are raised only to be dashed.

Worst of all, perhaps, is when you realize that you are the one not meeting others' expectations. The fact is, though, that you aren't here to live up to what others think of you. Jesus didn't; in part, that's why they killed him. But he did meet God's expectations for his life, which was all that really mattered.

Because God's kingdom is so great, God does have great expectations for any who would enter, and you should not take them lightly. What the world expects from you is of no importance; what God expects from you is paramount.

I was left alone in the beginning [because] not only did nobody know me, they didn't want to know me.
  -- Vince Dooley on not meeting the expectations of a 'name' coach

You have little if anything to gain from meeting the world's expectations of you; you have all of eternity to gain from meeting God's.

DAY 46

THE LEADER

Read Matthew 16:18-23.

"You are Peter, and on this rock I will build my church, and the gates of Hades will not overcome it" (v. 18).

For a while, Vance Cuff wasn't sure he would even be admitted into UGA. After that rocky start, though, he went on to become a leader for the Dawgs both on the field and in the classroom.

"I was terrified," Cuff said in recalling the way he felt in the fall of 2007. At the time, the SuperPrep All-American cornerback from Moultrie was sweating out getting into Georgia. The NCAA had some questions about a speech class he took in high school. Thus, Cuff spent much of that summer wondering if he would even be in college, let alone playing football. Only two days before UGA's camp started, Cuff got the word: He was in.

He took the lesson of his uncertainty to heart, making both the Athletic Director's Honor Roll and the Dean's List while he was in Athens. He graduated on time in May 2010.

Cuff didn't emerge as a leader just in the classroom. He played almost as soon as he showed up, a regular in the Dawgs' cornerback rotation. In the spring of 2010, prior to his senior season, he established himself as a team leader when he ran the fastest 40-yard dash on the squad. "It looked like he was shot out of a cannon," cornerback Brandon Boykin said about Cuff's 4.24 sprint.

Cuff also was a solid leader with his attitude. As the Bulldogs' only senior cornerback, he knew he had to set the example because

BULLDOGS

the coaches and the freshmen were watching him. He recalled his own experience as a freshman, watching some seniors lean over because they were tired. "When I'm tired, I know [the freshmen] are watching so I stay up and try to keep guys up," he said.

In 2010, Cuff the leader appeared in every game and led the team with five pass break-ups. He used his speed to return an interception for a touchdown in the 55-7 win over Idaho State.

Every aspect of life that involves people – every organization, every group, every project, every team -- must have a leader like Vance Cuff. If goals are to be reached, somebody must take charge.

The early Christian church was no different. Jesus knew this, so he designated the leader in Simon Peter, who was such an unlikely choice to assume such an awesome, world-changing responsibility that Jesus soon after rebuked him as "Satan."

In *Twelve Ordinary Men*, John MacArthur described Simon as "ambivalent, vacillating, impulsive, unsubmissive." Hardly a man to inspire confidence in his leadership skills. Yet, according to MacArthur, Peter became "the greatest preacher among the apostles" and the "dominant figure" in the birth of the church.

The implication for your own life is both obvious and unsettling. You may think you lack the attributes necessary to make a good leader for Christ. But consider Simon Peter, an ordinary man who allowed Christ to rule his life and became the foundation upon which the Christian church was built.

It's about keeping the team up and setting an example.
-- Vance Cuff on leadership

God's leaders are men and women
who allow Jesus to lead them.

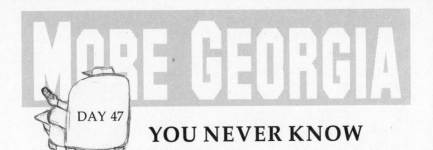

DAY 47

YOU NEVER KNOW

Read Acts 26:1-20.

"'[I]n all Judea, and to the Gentiles also, I preached that they should repent and turn to God'" (v. 20).

If a youngster is athletic growing up, you just never know what sport he may be interested in. Take John Jenkins, for instance.

Jenkins came to Georgia as a junior college transfer in 2011, filling an immediate need for a big nose tackle in the Bulldogs' new 3-4 defense. He was second-team All-SEC in 2012. At 6-foot-3 and 351 lbs. as a Bulldog, Jenkins was a mountain of a man. He was also so remarkably quick on his feet that when defensive end Abry Jones was injured, Jenkins moved over and filled in.

Jenkins grew up big. His mother frequently reminded him not to drop himself into a chair but to lower himself into it to protect the springs. Still, he once broke his mother's bed just by sitting on it. As he kept growing, he would look at the furniture before he sat down, and if he had any doubts, he'd just stand.

So naturally, as a big, athletic kid growing up in Connecticut, Jenkins played some sports. He played football and basketball, but "the one sport I was actually good at," he said -- well, you just never know about that one. It was BMX racing. This really big man who was a really big kid was a bike rider.

"That's for real," his mother said. "We were out racing those bikes about every weekend and he was winning all kinds of trophies. . . . He used to blow them away on the BMX track." Jenkins' mom conceded that her son was the biggest kid on the course and some of the other riders were a little scared about racing him.

"I was better at [bike racing] than I was at football," Jenkins said. You never know.

You never know what you can do until – like big John Jenkins and bike racing -- you want to bad enough or until – like Paul -- you have to because God insists. Serving in the military, maybe even in combat. Standing by a friend while everyone else unjustly excoriates her. Undergoing agonizing medical treatment and managing to smile. You never know what life will demand of you.

It's that way too in your relationship with God. As Paul, the most persistent persecutor of first-century Christians, discovered, you never know what God will ask of you. You can know, however, that God expects you to be faithful; thus, you must be willing to trust him even when he calls you to tasks that appear daunting and beyond your abilities.

You can respond faithfully and confidently to whatever God calls you to do for him. That's because even though you never know what lies ahead, you can know with absolutely certainty that God will lead you and will provide what you need. As it was with the Israelites, God will never lead you into the wilderness and then leave you there.

I don't know what bike he's riding. I'm not sure there's one that could hold him.
– UGA linebacker Christian Robinson on John Jenkins' bike racing

You never know what God will ask you to do,
but you always know he will provide everything
you need to do it.

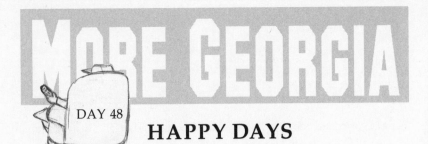

DAY 48

HAPPY DAYS

Read Nehemiah 8:1-3, 9-12.

"'Do not grieve, for the joy of the Lord is your strength'"
(v. 10b).

For David Greene, playing football was never about the glory and the honors, but the simple happiness of the moment. When he couldn't find that anymore, he left the game.

When Greene ended his career in Athens after the 2004 season, he was the winningest quarterback in NCAA history; his career total of 41 wins is still the most for a Bulldog. He threw for 11,528 yards, an SEC record at the time. He set a school record with 72 passing touchdowns, broken by Aaron Murray. He led the Dogs to the 2002 SEC title and a return trip to the title game in 2003.

Greene received more than his share of honors and fame. For instance, he was the SEC's Offensive Rookie of the Year in 2001 and the Offensive Player of the Year in 2002. All that success, however, didn't translate into a career in the NFL. Greene was drafted in the fourth round in 2005 and spent three seasons in the pros. He never, however, played a single down during the regular season.

Why not? Perhaps because of the reason why Greene was so successful in high school and at Georgia: He played for the moment, for the happiness he found in beating Tennessee in 2001 with the hobnailed boot pass to Verron Haynes. (See Devotion No. 89.) He played for a university that he loved. He didn't find that

BULLDOGS

same happiness in the pro game.

"I just never enjoyed it that much," he said. "I love watching the NFL, . . . but [it] didn't have the camaraderie of college, there's so much turnover."

So after the 2008 season, Greene walked away from the game to find his happy days elsewhere. "Once I made the decision, I was 100 percent at peace," he said.

A widespread theology preaches that happiness and prosperity are signs of faithfulness. It's certainly seductive, this notion that with faith comes happiness.

But it reduces God to a servant or a vending machine existing only to meet our wishes, coughing up whatever it takes to make us happy. This theology also means that if I am not happy, then God has failed.

Yes, God wants us to be happy. God gave us our life to enjoy; God created this world for us to enjoy; he sure doesn't need it. In God's economy, though, we are to be happy but only with conditions. If sin makes us happy, God doesn't want it for our lives. Moreover, if some thing in our lives, some circumstance in our lives, or even some person in our lives makes us happy, then God is indifferent about it.

God is so good to us that he wants more for us than happiness, which is temporal and worldly. For us, he wants joy, which is eternal and divine, and is found only in God through Jesus Christ.

I just loved the feel of college and high school ball.
*   -- David Greene on the happiness he found in playing football*

Happiness simply isn't good enough for us
because it doesn't depend upon Jesus Christ.

DAY 49

THE INTERVIEW

Read Romans 14: 1-12.

"We will all stand before God's judgment seat. . . . So then, each of us will give an account of himself to God" (vv. 10, 12).

Meghan Boenig nearly blew her job interview at UGA before she ever even said a word.

Boenig is one of the most successful head coaches in Georgia athletic history. As the only boss the UGA equestrian program has ever had since its inception as a varsity sport in 2002-03, she won five national titles and six Southern titles -- the equivalent of the SEC crown -- through the 2011-12 season. During that time, the team rode to an astonishing 44-1 dual meet record at home. The program has been so successful that Boenig practically has her pick of the nation's best riders. For instance, Emma Lipman of Bedford, N.Y., and a senior in 2012-13, said, "I didn't look at any other school to ride at when I was recruited. This is a program that everyone wants to be part of."

But the program didn't exist when Boenig, 24 years old and fresh out of graduate school at Texas A&M, showed up for her interview in 2001. And she made a mistake that those she was trying to impress quickly noticed: She wore a coral-colored shirt.

"It was much more pink," she protested. To her interviewers, however, the shirt bore a definite orange tint, a serious taboo in the land of rivals such as Florida, Tennessee, and Auburn. "When they called me back [for a second interview]," Boenig said, "I had red on that day."

Once the interviewers recovered from the shock of Boenig's shirt, they had only one real concern. Then-athletic director Vince Dooley expressed it, saying, "You're awfully young to be taking all of this on, aren't you?" "Coach," she replied, "if this program is successful, then I'm always going to be successful."

Good enough. In October 2001, Boenig became the university's youngest head coach -- and she has been successful ever since.

You've experienced the stress, the anxiety, the helpless feeling that's inevitably a part of any job interview. You tried to appear calm and relaxed while struggling to come up with reasonably original answers to banal questions and to hide your considered opinion that the interviewer was a total geek. You told yourself that if they turned you down, it was their loss.

You won't be so indifferent or nonchalant, though, about your last interview: the one with God. A day will come when we will all stand before God to account for ourselves. It is to God and God alone – not our friends, not our parents, not society in general – that we must give a final and complete account.

Since all eternity will be at stake, it sure would help to have a surefire reference with you. One – and only one -- is available: Jesus Christ.

I was all red and black.
-- Meghan Boenig on her attire at her follow-up interview

You will have one last interview -- with God
-- and you certainly want Jesus there with you
as a character witness.

DAY 50

FOOD FOR THOUGHT

Read Genesis 9:1-7.

*"Everything that lives and moves will be food for you. Just
as I gave you the green plants, I now give you everything"*
(v. 3).

Joe Tereshinski, Sr., had a clear priority when he showed up to
play football for the Dawgs: wolf down a whole lot of food.

When head coach Wally Butts and assistant coach Bill Hartman
visited Tereshinski's home in Pennsylvania for a recruiting visit,
the youngster was worried about his weight since he was never
heavier than 162 pounds in high school. So to make himself look
bigger, he put on two bulky sweaters and topped them off with a
heavyweight basketball jacket for his meeting with the coaches.

Tereshinski also got some unexpected help with his problem
from a former Bulldog star. Harold "War Eagle" Ketron was a lineman for Georgia from 1901-03 and 1906 who was involved in Tereshinski's recruiting and who was at the meeting with the coaches.
When Butts asked the senior how much he weighed, the former
Bulldog captain spoke right up: 186 pounds. "I didn't correct him,"
Tereshinski said.

Once the rookie arrived in Athens, though, the scales wouldn't
lie for him; they said 162 pounds. When coaches asked what
happened to all that weight, Tereshinski came up with a whopper
of his own. He told them he had been sick.

After Tereshinski's first scrimmage, Butts told him they had been considering sending him to a prep school to put on some weight. "But I watched you on every play during the scrimmage," Butts said. "Anybody who wants to play football as badly as you've shown me . . . well you can stay as long as you wish."

Tereshinski did. He gained enough weight to be an All-SEC end in 1946 and play eight seasons in the pros.

Belly up to the buffet, boys and girls, for barbecue, sirloin steak, grilled chicken, and fried catfish with hush puppies and cheese grits. Rachael Ray is a household name; hamburger joints, pizza parlors, and taco stands lurk on every corner; and we have a TV channel devoted exclusively to food. We love our chow.

Food is one of God's really good ideas, but consider the complex divine plan that begins with a kernel and winds up with corn-on-the-cob slathered with butter and littered with salt. The creator of all life devised a downright fascinating and effective system in which living things are sustained and nourished physically through the sacrifice of other living things in a way similar to what Christ underwent to save us spiritually.

Whether it's fast food or home-cooked, practically everything we eat is a gift from God secured through a divine plan in which some plants and/or animals have given up their lives. Pausing to give thanks before we dive in seems the least we can do.

I started eating the good food they served us at the dorm and started gaining some weight.

-- Joe Tereshinski, Sr.

**God created a system that nourishes us
through the sacrifice of other living things;
that's worth a thank-you.**

DAY 51

SIGHT UNSEEN

Read 2 Corinthians 5:1-10.

"We live by faith, not by sight" (v. 7).

Because an All-SEC linebacker who was sidelined by an injury saw something no one else did, the offense executed a key play in one of the greatest drives in Dawg history.

Chip Wisdom was a three-year starter (1969-71) for the Dawgs and an All-SEC linebacker in 1971. He was a Bulldog assistant coach from 1972-80. His senior year the Dawgs went 11-1, losing only to Auburn and Pat Sullivan 35-20 in a battle of unbeatens.

The regular season ended Thanksgiving night against Georgia Tech before a national TV audience. Tech was only 6-4 while the Dawgs were ranked 7th in the nation. Nevertheless, with only 89 seconds left to play, UGA was in deep trouble, trailing 24-21 and sitting at its own 35.

The trouble got even deeper than that. With 57 seconds left, the Dawgs faced fourth-and-ten at the Jacket 43. But sophomore quarterback Andy Johnson found end tight end Mike Green over the middle for 18 yards. He then hit split end Lynn Hunnicutt with a pair of passes down to the 9 with 31 seconds on the clock.

After Johnson was sacked at the 13, UGA called its final time out. 28 seconds. Johnson trotted over to the sideline to confer with his coaches. Wisdom was right there with them; he didn't play because of a knee injury. The coaches couldn't decide on a call until backup quarterback James Ray shouted, "Let [senior flanker

BULLDOGS

Jimmy] Shirer run that down-and-out that has been working so well." That was the call. Johnson headed out to the huddle.

Right about then, Wisdom glanced around and discovered to his dismay that Shirer was standing next to him. He hadn't heard the play call and thus wasn't in the game. Wisdom grabbed him and hollered, "Jimmy, go in there and run that out route."

Shirer did and Johnson threw a strike to the 1. Jimmy Poulos went up and over on the next play with 14 seconds left. Thanks in large part to something Chip Wisdom saw, UGA had a 28-24 win.

To close our eyes or to be engulfed suddenly by total darkness plunges us into a world in which we struggle to function. Our world and our place in it are built on our eyesight, so much so that we tout "Seeing is believing." If we can't see it, we don't believe it. Perhaps the most famous proponent of this attitude was the disciple Thomas, who refused to believe Jesus had risen from the dead until he saw the proof for himself.

But our sight carries us only so far because its usefulness is restricted to the physical world. Eyesight has no place in spiritual matters. We don't "see" God; we don't "see" Jesus; we don't "see" God at work in the physical world. And yet we know God; we know Jesus; we know God is in control. We "know" all that because as the children of God, we live by faith and not by sight.

Looking through the eyes of faith, we understand that believing is seeing.

I managed to contribute a little bit to our win.
-- Chip Wisdom on his seeing Jimmy Shirer on the sideline

In God's physical world, seeing is believing;
in God's spiritual world, believing is seeing.

DAY 52

SMILING FACES

Read Isaiah 35.

"[E]verlasting joy will crown their heads. Gladness and joy will overtake them" (v. 10).

One of the most gentle of the Bulldogs often had teammates scared to death of him -- because he wouldn't smile.

DeAngelo Tyson played in fifty games from 2008-2011, starting every game he appeared in but one his junior and senior seasons. He started at nose guard in 2010 and then moved to his natural position, defensive end, as a senior. He won a coaches' leadership award and appeared in the East-West Shrine Game in 2011.

Tyson was moved out of position in 2010 for one reason: "He was the best option we had," said defensive line coach Rodney Garner. The development of Kwame Geathers and the arrival of Jonathan Jenkins freed Tyson up to move back to end in 2011.

All the while, many of Tyson's fellow Bulldogs were, as receiver Tavarres King admitted, "kind of scared of him." Center Ben Jones agreed. "He was a little scary. I was wondering if he wanted to kill me every day." The reason for their discomfiture went beyond Tyson's imposing stature: 6-foot-2, 306 lbs.

He was scary because he rarely, if ever, smiled. The natural frown into which his face relaxed and the even disposition that characterized him meant he rarely changed expression.

But when Jones and his teammates got to know Tyson and could see past the frown, they discovered one of their favorite

BULLDOGS

people. "He's a great guy and he's the kind of guy you want at your side on Saturday," King said. But then he added, "I can't remember the last time I saw him smile." Tackle Cordy Glenn, who was Tyson's roommate, actually saw him smile more than once. "I know he smiles when we get done with workouts and stuff like that," he said.

Tyson had a monster game in the 42-34 win over Georgia Tech in 2010 with sixteen tackles. Naturally, he made all those plays and wreaked all that havoc without cracking a smile.

What does your smile say about you? What is it that makes you smile and laugh in the first place? Your dad's corny jokes? Don Knotts as Barney Fife. Your pal's bad imitations? A Bulldog TD?

When you smile, the ones who love you and whom you love can't help but return the favor -- and the joy. It's like turning on a bright light in a world threatened by darkness.

Besides, you have good reason to walk around all the time with a smile on your face -- not because of something you have done but rather because of what God has done for you. As a result of his great love for you, God acted through Jesus to give you free and eternal salvation. That should certainly make you smile.

But there's more. Jesus isn't through with this fallen world. One day he will return, and Heaven on Earth will become a reality. We'll be right there with him to share it all.

Basking in his glory, we'll be smiling the whole time.

I'm not the type of guy who's going to smile all the time.
-- DeAngelo Tyson

It's so overused it's become a cliché,
but it's true nevertheless: Smile! God loves you.

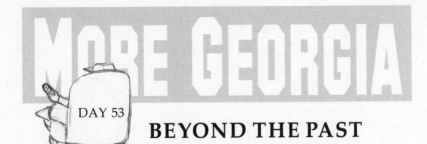

DAY 53

BEYOND THE PAST

Read Colossians 3:1-10.

"You used to walk in these ways, in the life you once lived. But now you must rid yourself of all such things" (vv. 7, 8a).

Here's a real blast from the past we aren't likely to ever see again: The entire Florida State student body once turned out to cheer for the Gators against the Dawgs.

In 1931, Georgia and Florida met in Jacksonville for the first time, a reminder of the time long past when the game searched for a permanent home. Among those cheering on the Gators were all the girls from Florida State College for Women in Tallahassee, which would eventually turn coed as FSU.

Coached by Harry Mehre, this Dawg team from the past was packed with stars. Quarterback Spud Chandler would pitch for the Yankees and win the AL's MVP award in 1943. Three-time All-Southern Conference end Vernon "Catfish" Smith was so sensational that he would be elected to the College Football Hall of Fame in 1979. Other outstanding Bulldogs that season included All-Southern guard Red Leathers, running back Homer Key, and All-Southern fullback Jack Roberts.

And then there was Norman "Buster" Mott. In his first-ever collegiate game, against Oglethorpe, he scored long touchdowns the first three times he touched the ball. That netted him a mention in *Ripley's Believe It or Not*. The flamboyant Mott, who earned a reputation as quite a party guy, subsequently announced upon his arrival at any gathering, "Believe it or not, it's Buster Mott."

On this day, the Gators didn't believe what they saw. Georgia stomped them. Mott enhanced his reputation with a 56-yard run for a TD in the second quarter, and Georgia jumped out to a 20-0 halftime lead. In the last half, Key and Joseph Whire scored as the Dogs romped to a 33-6 lead win.

The past often seems quaint to us. Imagine FSU coeds cheering robustly for the Gators today or the Georgia-Florida game being played in Macon, Savannah, or Tampa as it once was.

But in our personal lives, the past usually isn't quaint at all. Instead, it often haunts us like a ghost. We lug around our regrets and memories of our past failures, omissions, and shortcomings, donning them each day as we do our clothes.

Short of utter callousness and severe memory problems, only one way exists to free ourselves totally from the past: the change offered through salvation in Jesus Christ. Even when we fall on our knees in despair and cry out to Jesus, we sometimes falsely believe that salvation and forgiveness can never be ours. That's because many desperate seekers fall prey to the fallacy that they must be perfect before Jesus will accept them. The truth is that we need Jesus because we are not perfect.

Jesus didn't die for our past but for our future. He died to free us from the past and to replace it with a glorious future.

The minute I think about past letdowns or future hypotheticals, I mentally put myself on shaky ground.
-- Olympic Alpine skier Julia Mancuso

Every saint has a past; every sinner has a future.

HANGING IN THERE

Read Mark 14:32-42.

"'Father,' he said, 'everything is possible for you. Take this cup from me. Yet not what I will, but what you will'" (v. 36).

Hungry for a win, the Lady Bulldogs seemed to have one with a buzzer-beating shot. So what do you do when the rule book takes the win away? If you're Georgia, you just keep after it.

Andy Landers' Dogs of 2010-11 went 23-11 and advanced to the Sweet 16 in the NCAA Tournament. (See Devotion No. 6.) On Feb. 3, though, they needed a win coming off a rough road trip. They got it, but they had to earn it twice.

The team hosted Arkansas after dropping its first conference games of the season. "We needed to get some pep back in our step after losing two straight," said guard Meredith Mitchell. But the 16-5 Razorbacks weren't at all cooperative. Their defense limited the Dawgs to 20 points in the first half; Georgia didn't take its first lead until 18:48 remained in the game.

The Lady Bulldogs hung in there, however, by playing some tough defense of their own. They held Arkansas to 35 percent shooting, and the two teams grimly slugged it out into the final second. With the score tied at 47 with 0.3 on the clock, Georgia inbounded the ball to freshman guard Khaalidah Miller, who hit a three pointer for an apparent Bulldog win.

The referees put a sudden halt to the celebration, however. They

BULLDOGS

cited an NCAA rule that says the only legal shot in the last 0.3 seconds of a game is a tip and waved off Miller's trey. Overtime.

A win they needed badly had been snatched away from them, but the Dawgs wouldn't give in. With 33 seconds left in the extra period, Arkansas tied the game at 54. With 13 seconds left, sophomore forward Jasmine Hassell grabbed an offensive rebound and was fouled. She hit the second free throw to give Georgia the lead All-SEC forward Porsha Phillips then stole a pass and hit a pair of charity shots when she was fouled.

The persistent Lady Bulldogs had a 57-54 win.

Life is tough; it inevitably beats us up and kicks us around some. But life has four quarters, and so here we are, still standing, still in the game. Like the Lady Bulldogs, we know that we can never win if we don't finish. We emerge as winners and champions only if we never give up, if we just see it through.

Interestingly, Jesus has been in the same situation. On that awful night in the garden, Jesus understood the nature of the suffering he was about to undergo, and he begged God to take it from him. In the end, though, he yielded to God's will and surrendered his own.

Even in the matter of persistence, Jesus is our example. As he did, we push doggedly and determinedly ahead – following God's will for our lives -- no matter how hard it gets. And we can do it because God is with us.

We were able to stay the course and get the win.
– Guard Jasmine James on the win over Arkansas

It's tough to keep going no matter what,
but you have God's power to help you through.

DAY 55

ANIMAL MAGNETISM

Read Psalm 139:1-18.

"For you created my inmost being; you knit me together in my mother's womb. I praise you because I am fearfully and wonderfully made" (vv. 13-14).

Sports *Illustrated* in 1997 famously called Uga the nation's best college mascot. In reality the magazine was quite a bit tardy with the declaration; after all, how many mascots ever actually play a part in a win as Uga III did in 1978?

Picked by one forecaster to battle Vanderbilt for the SEC cellar, the Dawgs traveled to LSU on Oct. 14 with a 3-1 record. Nevertheless, they were big underdogs to the 11th-ranked and unbeaten Tigers. But UGA had a twelfth Bulldog on its side -- Uga III -- who Vince Dooley always said helped his team that night.

Certainly, LSU's mascot, Mike the Bengal tiger, is an impressive sight. One of the school's more stirring pregame traditions is to circle the field with the cheerleaders riding atop Mike's cage, which is pulled by a truck. When the truck stops, the cheerleaders hop down and beat on the cage, thereby inciting a frenzied Mike to roar into a microphone.

On this night, Uga III stood at midfield, directly in Mike's path, and stolidly refused to budge. The big cat ran to the front of the cage and let fly with a mighty roar. As sportswriter Ron Higgins put it, "Uga III was not impressed and didn't even blink." Enraged, Mike raised up on his hind legs to rattle the cage before turning

BULLDOGS

loose "his angriest, scariest roar."

A fascinated Dooley was watching the whole showdown. After Mike roared a second time, according to Dooley, "Uga raises up, takes a couple of steps forward and barks." Mike immediately retreated to the back of his cage, cowering.

The excited head coach rushed to the dressing room to tell his players that Uga had faced down a Bengal tiger. "I said, 'Let's go, men, we got 'em tonight.'" They did; the Dogs matched their mascot's fighting spirit and won 24-17.

Animals such as Uga elicit our awe and our respect. Nothing enlivens a trip more than glimpsing turkeys, bears, or deer in the wild. Admit it: You go along with the kids' trip to the zoo because you think it's a cool place too. All that variety of life is mind-boggling. Who could conceive of a bulldog, a walrus, a moose, or a tiger? Who could possibly have that rich an imagination?

But the next time you're in a crowd, look around at the parade of faces. Who could come up with the idea for all those different people? For that matter, who could conceive of you? You are unique, a masterpiece who will never be duplicated.

The master creator, God Almighty, is behind it all. He thought of you and brought you into being. If you had a manufacturer's label, it might say, "Lovingly, fearfully, and wonderfully handmade in Heaven by #1 -- God."

I was so excited I couldn't wait to tell our team what I saw.
-- Vince Dooley on Uga and Mike

**You may consider a painting or
a magnificent animal to be a work of art,
but the real masterpiece is you.**

DAY 56

HOMELESS

Read Matthew 8:18-22.

"Jesus replied, 'Foxes have holes and birds of the air have nests, but the Son of Man has no place to lay his head'"
(v. 20).

Homeless since he was 9, he was sleeping in his car. And yet he made a crucial play in the Dogs' march to the 2002 SEC title.

Tony Milton was only 9 when he left home to stay with whoever would take him in. Despite the adversity, he starred in football in high school and was recruited by several schools, including FSU and its offensive coordinator, Mark Richt.

Milton couldn't quality for a scholarship, however, so he found work at a hotel. Often penniless, he frequently slept in his car. He was going nowhere until he decided to give football another try. He remembered that coach from FSU who had recruited him and learned he was now the rookie head man in Athens. He asked Richt if he could try out for the football team. When Richt asked him what position he wanted to play, Milton replied, "Coach, I don't care what I play. I just want a chance to be somebody."

Tony Milton wound up a somebody indeed. He walked on and made the team. A hamstring injury led to a redshirt season in 2001, and he began the 2002 season for the eventual SEC champs as the number-two tailback behind Musa Smith.

In the showdown against tenth-ranked Tennessee on Oct. 12, the Dogs led only 18-13 with 1:43 left. They faced fourth-and-two

BULLDOGS

at the Vols' 35. Richt went for it and called for a toss sweep. That meant Milton since Smith was injured. He romped for 25 yards to clinch the win amid what one writer called "the loudest I've probably heard Sanford Stadium during one single play."

With the emergence of other tailbacks, Milton's playing time gradually decreased over his final three seasons. But he graduated from UGA, and that homeless young man who only wanted to be somebody is part of Bulldog lore. He is somebody indeed.

Rock bottom in America has a face: the bag lady pushing a shopping cart; the scruffy guy with a beard and a backpack at the interstate exit holding a cardboard sign. Look closer at that bag lady or that scruffy guy, though, and you may see desperate women with children fleeing violence, veterans haunted by their combat experiences, or sick or injured workers.

Few of us are indifferent to the homeless. They often raise quite strong passions, whether we regard them as a ministry or an odorous nuisance. They trouble us, perhaps because we realize that we're only one catastrophic illness and a few paychecks away from joining them. They remind us of how tenuous our own hold upon material success really is.

But they also stir our compassion because we serve a Lord who – like them -- had no home, and for whom, the homeless, too, are his children.

Hey, coming from where I come from, that was luxury. My car had leather seats.
                -- Tony Milton on being homeless and sleeping in his car

**Because they, too, are God's children,
the homeless merit our compassion, not our scorn.**

HOPE CHEST

Read Psalm 42.

"Put your hope in God, for I will yet praise him, my Savior and my God" (v. 5b).

Hope did not spring eternal on the Georgia sideline as the clock ticked away in the 1980 Florida game.

Midway through the fourth quarter of that memorable day, Florida kicked a field goal to go up 21-20. Georgia punted and Florida ran some clock with a pair of first downs before kicking the ball back. With only 1:35 left, the Dawgs sat on their own 8.

As head coach Vince Dooley later wrote, some of the players "maintained hope born of youthful optimism," but at the same time "there was a feeling of having blown a tremendous opportunity." That "opportunity," of course, was Georgia's shot at the national title. The Dogs entered the game on Nov. 8 ranked no. 2 behind Notre Dame, which was tied that day by Georgia Tech.

"I remember feeling total disgust," said defensive guard Joe Creamons, who was from Eustis, Fla. "I couldn't believe we were going to lose to those guys."

Some players, including Herschel Walker, did remain hopeful. "I didn't think that we were going to lose that game," he said. "It ain't over. It ain't over yet," injured center Hugh Nall repeated.

Many, however, shared Creamons' disappointment. "I could just see the dream being shot down," said safety Jeff Hipp, a second-team All-America that year. Others, like defensive end

BULLDOGS

Pat McShea wavered. "I had not completely given up, but I was not feeling too good," he said. "It was looking real doubtful."

It was looking even more doubtful after the offense ran two plays and lost a yard. Center Joe Happe said it felt like "third and a million." But then came the most famous play in Georgia football history, Buck Belue to Lindsay Scott.

Hope was restored.

Only when a life has no hope does it become not worth the living. To hope is not merely to want something; that is desire or wishful thinking. Desire must be coupled with some degree of expectation to produce hope.

Therein lies the great problem. We may well wish for a million dollars, relief from our diabetes, world peace, or a safe way to lose weight while stuffing ourselves with doughnuts and fried chicken. Our hopes, however, must be firmly grounded, or they will inevitably lead us to disappointment, shame, and disaster. In other words, false hopes ruin us.

One of the most basic issues of our lives, therefore, becomes discovering or locating that in which we can place our hope. Where can we find sure promises for a future that we can count on? Where can we place our hope along with the realistic expectation that we can live securely even though some of the promises we rely on are yet to be delivered?

In God. In God and God alone lies our hope.

I felt like we had blown our undefeated hopes.
-- Senior safety Bob Kelly, late in the '80 Florida game

God and his sustaining power are the source of the only meaningful hope possible in our lives.

DAY 58

A LONG SHOT

Read Matthew 9:9-13.

"[Jesus] saw a man named Matthew sitting at the tax
collector's booth. 'Follow me,' he told him, and Matthew
got up and followed him" (v. 9).

Talk about your long shot to be hired as a coach. She didn't
apply for the job, the school's star athlete didn't want her, and
the school was considering doing away with her sport altogether.
The long shot was Suzanne Yoculan.

From 1984-2009, Yoculan coached the Dawgs to ten national
titles and sixteen SEC crowns. She was the National Coach of the
Year five times, ending her career with a record of 836-117-7.

After quitting the Penn State gymnastics squad without ever
competing in a meet, Yoculan began to teach the sport. She applied
for the head coaching spot at Nebraska in 1984 and didn't even
rate an interview. "I was devastated," she said. The Huskers hired
the Georgia coach, who fired a broadside as he left by saying the
program had no support from the administration. He was right;
at the time, the school was considering dropping gymnastics.

Fed up by the rejection, Yoculan had no intention of applying
for the Georgia job. But gym owner and long-time friend Ed Isa-
belle forged her signature on an application. Thus, Yoculan was
quite surprised when Liz Murphey, UGA's senior administrator
for the women's programs, called her up. Murphey had to talk
Yoculan into coming for an interview, but one visit to the campus

changed the future Hall-of-Famer's mind.

Senior Kathy McMinn, UGA's first four-time All America in a women's sport and a member of the search committee, wasn't too keen, however, on the idea of a female coach. "I just don't think that's gonna work," she told Murphey. Then she saw Yoculan in the gym with the men's team. McMinn, who "knew more about women's gymnastics than anyone else on campus," was instrumental in persuading AD Vince Dooley not to axe the sport.

Suzanne Yoculan the long shot got the job. The rest is history.

Matthew the tax collector was another long shot, an unlikely person to be a confidant of the Son of God. While we may not get all warm and fuzzy about the IRS, our government's revenue agents are nothing like Matthew and his ilk. He bought a franchise, paying the Roman Empire for the privilege of extorting, bullying, and stealing everything he could from his own people. John MacArthur called tax collectors of the time "despicable, vile, unprincipled scoundrels."

And yet, Jesus said only two words to this lowlife: "Follow me." Jesus knew that this long shot would make an excellent disciple.

It's the same with us. While we may not be quite as vile as Matthew was, none of us can stand before God with our hands clean and our hearts pure. We are all impossibly long shots to enter God's Heaven. That is, until we do what Matthew did: get up and follow Jesus.

I'm not interested. I did not even apply.
-- Suzanne Yoculan to Liz Murphey on the UGA job

**Jesus changes us from being long shots
to enter God's Kingdom to being sure things.**

REVELATION

Read Isaiah 53.

"But he was pierced for our transgressions, he was crushed for our iniquities; the punishment that brought us peace was upon him, and by his wounds we are healed" (v. 5).

When it came to Kent Lawrence and the Cotton Bowl, a couple of Bulldog legends had a bit of the prophet in them.

On Dec. 31, 1966, Vince Dooley's first SEC champions met SMU, champions of the Southwest Conference, in the Cotton Bowl. That 10-1 team featured All-Americans George Patton, Bill Stanfill, Edgar Chandler, and Lynn Hughes, and All-SEC picks Larry Kohn, Don Hayes, Ronnie Jenkins, and Bobby Etter. As the game began, however, the talk in the press box was about Lawrence, the Dogs' sophomore halfback.

Longtime UGA sports information director (and tennis coaching legend) Dan Magill was seated between Harry Mehre, who coached the Dogs for ten seasons (1928-37), and Blackie Sherrod of the *Dallas News*. Magill got the conversation started when he informed Sherrod that Lawrence was the fastest ball-carrier in UGA football history. He had run the 100 in 9.3 seconds and in a few weeks would beat O.J. Simpson in the NCAA Indoor 60-yard dash. After Magill's comment, Mehre added, "I have never seen a halfback with more speed and agility than Lawrence."

As if on cue, on the third play of the game, Lawrence took a

BULLDOGS

hand-off from quarterback Kirby Moore and hit a hole behind Jenkins. He broke to his left behind a block from Chandler and took off. Nobody could catch him; he went 74 yards for the touchdown, making prophets out of Magill and Mehre.

SMU never recovered and Georgia won easily 24-9. Lawrence went on to set the school record for rushing yards in a bowl game with 149, a mark later broken by Garrison Hearst (1993 Citrus) and Robert Edwards (2000 Outback) with 163 yards.

In our jaded age, we have pretty much relegated prophecy to dark rooms in which mysterious women peer into crystal balls or clasp our sweaty palms while uttering some vague generalities. At best, we understand a prophet as someone who predicts future events as Dan Magill and Harry Mehre seemed to do.

Within the pages of the Bible, though, we encounter something radically different. A prophet is a messenger from God, one who relays divine revelation to others.

Prophets seem somewhat foreign to us because in one very real sense the age of prophecy is over. In the name of Jesus, we have access to God through our prayers and through scripture. In searching for God's will for our lives, we seek divine revelation. We may speak only for ourselves and not for the greater body of Christ, but we do not need a prophet to discern what God would have us do. We need faith in the one whose birth, life, and death fulfilled more than 300 Bible prophecies.

I see what you mean!
    -- Blackie Sherrod after Kent Lawrence's 74-yard touchdown run

**Persons of faith continuously seek
a word from God for their lives.**

DAY 60

WANT ADS

Read Psalm 73:23-28.

"Whom have I in heaven but you? And earth has nothing I desire besides you" (v. 25).

Kris Durham was pretty realistic about the NFL draft. All he wanted was to hear his name called. Funny thing about that.

As the 6'-5" wide receiver entered his senior season at UGA in 2010, the notion that he would be picked in any round of the draft was pretty far-fetched. He had a grand total of thirty-two catches to show for four years in Athens and had lost the 2009 season to shoulder surgery. Even Durham didn't think too awfully much of his chances; he spent the spring prior to his senior season teaching at a middle school, astutely preparing himself for life after football.

But when the Dawgs' star receiver, A.J. Green, was suspended for four games to start the 2010 season, Durham unexpectedly became freshman quarterback Aaron Murray's go-to guy. He finished the season with 32 catches for 659 yards and three touchdowns, including two 100-yard games.

Still, that showing didn't earn him a spot among the 300-plus prospects invited to the NFL combine. He received his first real notice with a 4.3 40-yard dash at UGA's pro day in March 2011. His stock rose and he worked out for several different teams.

On draft day, Durham was prepared to be patient. He said he just wanted to hear his name called, no matter what the round.

BULLDOGS

He got what he wanted and more. The Seattle Seahawks called his name -- in the fourth round; he was the twelfth receiver picked. He was taken higher than Terrence Edwards, Fred Gibson, and Brice Hunter, at the time three of UGA's top four in career receiving yards.

When Seattle cut him after training camp in 2012, Durham got something else he wanted. The Detroit Lions signed him, and he was reunited with his former roommate, Matthew Stafford.

What do you want out of life? A caring family, a home of your own, the respect of those whom you admire? Our heart's desires can elevate us to greatness and goodness, but they can also plunge us into destruction, despair, and evil. Drugs, alcohol, control, sex, power, worldly success: Do these desires motivate you?

Desires are not inherently evil or bad for you; after all, God planted the capacity to desire in us. The key is determining which of your heart's desires are healthful and are worth pursuing and which are dangerous and are best avoided.

Not surprisingly, the answer to the dilemma lies with God. You consult the one whose own heart's desire is for what is unequivocally best for you, who is driven only by his unqualified love for you. You match what you want for yourself with what God wants for you. Your deepest heart's desire must be the establishment and maintenance of an intimate relationship with God.

I was speechless when it happened.
-- Kris Durham on getting what he wanted out of the 2011 draft

Whether our desires drive us to greatness
or to destruction is determined by whether
they are also God's desires for our lives.

DAY 61

TEST CASE

Read Genesis 39.

"But while Joseph was there in the prison, the Lord was with him" (vv. 20b-21a).

Oh, Lord," Khaalidah Miller said to herself when she realized she was about to be tested by playing a new position against one of the best teams in the country.

Miller moved into the Lady Bulldogs' starting lineup midway through her freshman season in 2009-10 and stayed there. On Feb. 3, 2013, she started her 71st game. They all had one thing in common: She was the team's shooting guard. Beside her in the backcourt was then-senior point guard Jasmine James, who for the last two seasons had led the team in assists.

As the 2012-13 season progressed, head coach Andy Landers practiced Miller some at point guard just in case of an emergency. That emergency arose after only a few practices under some really tough circumstances.

The opponent for Miller's 71st start was 8th-ranked Kentucky in Lexington. In this clash of 19-2 powerhouses, James picked up three fouls in the first half. Landers turned to his emergency plan, which elicited Miller's "Oh, Lord" response.

That initial reaction was certainly justified. Miller hadn't played the position seriously since high school. "I always kind of looked at [James] as the one to control the floor," she said. Moreover, Kentucky wasn't just good; the Cats had won 34 straight games on their home court. To make it worse, the 13th-ranked Dawgs were in trouble. At halftime, they trailed 40-30.

So did Miller pass her test? With flying colors. She poured in a career-high 25 points, and in her 34 minutes at point guard, she ran the offense with only two turnovers. The Bulldogs rallied to win a 75-71 thriller.

Life often seems to be just one battery of tests after another: high-school and college final exams, college entrance exams, the driver's license test, professional certification exams.

But it is the tests in our lives that don't involve paper and pen that often demand the most of us. That is, as it was with Khaalidah Miller suddenly against Kentucky, we regularly run headlong into challenges, obstacles, and barriers that test our abilities and our persistence and sometimes -- as with Joseph in prison in Egypt -- our faith.

Life itself is one long test, which means some parts are bound to be hard. In fact, the difficult circumstances of our lives most directly test and build our character and our faith.

Viewing life as an ongoing exam may help you preserve your sanity, your perspective, and your faith when you find yourself tested. After all, God is the proctor, but he isn't neutral. He even gave you the answer you need to pass life's test with flying colors; that answer is "Jesus."

With that answer, you don't get a grade; you get Heaven.

I've just been working it, and tonight was the night I had to step up and play the position.
> *-- Khaalidah Miller on playing point guard vs. Kentucky*

Life is a test that God wants you to ace.

DAY 62

TROUBLED TIMES

Read Nahum 1:1-8.

"The Lord is good, a refuge in times of trouble. He cares for those who trust in him" (v. 8).

The Dawgs were in deep trouble until a couple of troubled plays let them escape with a dramatic win over Georgia Tech.

On Dec. 2, 1978, in Athens, the 8-1-1 Bulldogs trailed 7-3 Tech 28-21 with 2:24 to play. On fourth down at the Jacket 42, freshman quarterback Buck Belue rolled out and immediately was in deep trouble from the Tech rush. Downfield, though, sophomore wide receiver Amp Arnold realized his quarterback's plight and broke his pattern, turning toward the goal line. He was open; Belue saw him and threw him a strike for a 42-yard touchdown.

That made it a 28-27 game, and head coach Vince Dooley went for the win with a pass to tight end Mark Hodge. The pass was incomplete, but yellow flags flew all over the place for an obvious pass interference call.

What now? Dooley figured the percentage call was to send tailback Willie McClendon over the top for the yard-and-a-half the Dawgs needed to take the lead. But offensive coordinator Bill Pace preferred a fake to McClendon with Belue running an option.

UGA was in trouble as the play clock ticked on while the two coaches disagreed. But because the headsets of the day didn't allow for open conversation, Pace acted on his own to avoid the delay-of-game penalty. He instructed Charley Whittemore, who signaled the plays to the quarterback, to run the option. "Time essentially ran out before the head coach had an opportunity to dictate his preference."

The fullback ran the wrong way on the play, which left a Tech cornerback with an open lane to Belue. He hit Belue but not cleanly, and Belue escaped trouble by pitching to Arnold, who waltzed into the end zone. Despite their trouble, Georgia had a 29-28 win.

For every football team in every game, trouble is gonna come. Winning or losing a game is largely determined by how a team handles the trouble that comes its way during the ebb and flow of the sixty minutes of action.

Life is no different. For each of us, trouble is gonna come. The decisive factor for us all is how we handle it. What do we do when we're in trouble?

Admittedly, some troubles are worse and are more devastating than others. From health problems to financial woes to family problems, trouble can change our lives and everything about it.

The most fearsome danger, though, lies not in what trouble can do to us physically, emotionally, or psychologically, but in its potential to affect us spiritually. Do we respond to it by turning to the profane or to the profound? Does trouble wreck our faith in God or strengthen our trust in him?

Like everything of this world, trouble is temporal; God's love and power, however, are not. In God, we have a sure and certain refuge during the troubled times of our lives.

I saw Buck was in trouble, I turned upfield.
-- Amp Arnold on his late TD against Tech in 1978

Trouble will come and God will be there for us.

DAY 63

AS A RULE

Read Luke 5:27-32.

*"Why do you eat and drink with tax collectors and
'sinners'?" (v. 30b)*

Derek Dooley so desperately wanted his dad to set aside one of
his most inviolate rules that he asked God for a blowout.

When Derek trotted onto the field at Neyland Stadium for the
opening game of the 2010 season, his dad and he became the first
father-son duo ever to be SEC head football coaches. At the time,
that little bit of history slipped by the elder Dooley, who has a
master's degree in history. That may be because he never really
expected his son to be a football coach.

But Derek couldn't stay away from the game he had literally
grown up with. The youngest of the Dooley clan had loved the
game even as "a pipsqueak," when that love drove him to convince his dad to break one of his hard-and-fast rules.

The head Bulldog had a firm rule that none of the kids could
go on the Georgia sideline during a game until they were 12 years
old. In 1975, 7-year-old Derek asked his dad if he could join him
on the field during the Georgia Tech game. Vince answered that
Derek could come to the sideline only if Georgia was winning big
at the end of the third quarter and only if he didn't bother him or
his players. The night before the game during the family's prayer
time, Derek prayed earnestly for a Bulldog blowout.

He got it. Georgia led 42-7 after three quarters, so Barbara Dooley escorted little Derek to the field and left him there. When Tech scored twice and was moving again, she noticed father and son exchanging some words in violation of the rule that dad had set up for the sideline visit. That night as the couple got ready for bed, Vince told Barbara that Derek had said to him, "Dad, don't worry about a thing. Jesus is just here having a little fun!"

Like 7-year-old Derek Dooley, you live by rules that others set up. Some lender determined the interest rate on your mortgage and your car loan. You work hours and shifts that somebody else established. Someone else decided what day your garbage gets picked up and what school district your house is in.

Jesus encountered societal rules also, including a strict set of religious edicts that dictated what company he should keep, what people, in other words, were fit for him to socialize with, talk to, or share a meal with. Jesus ignored the rules, choosing love instead of mindless obedience and demonstrating his disdain for society's rules by mingling with the outcasts, the lowlifes, the poor, and the misfits.

You, too, have to choose when you find yourself in the presence of someone whom society deems undesirable. Will you choose the rules or love?

Are you willing to be a rebel for love — as Jesus was for you?

The fewer rules a coach has, the fewer rules there are for players to break.

-- John Madden

**Society's rules dictate who is acceptable
and who is not, but love in the name of Jesus
knows no such distinctions.**

DAY 64

REDEEMED

Read 1 Peter 1:17-25.

"It was not with perishable things such as silver or gold that you were redeemed from the empty way of life handed down to you from your forefathers, but with the precious blood of Christ" (vv. 18-19).

After pulling off one of the most embarrassing plays in Georgia football history, Mikey Henderson needed some redemption.

Henderson's junior season of 2006 opened in Sanford Stadium against Western Kentucky. After the Bulldog defense held on the game's opening possession, he trotted onto the field for his first chance to return a punt. He gathered the ball in at the Georgia 34 and broke free. On his first-ever collegiate return, Henderson was on his way to a 66-yard touchdown.

In his excitement, though, he blew it. Only a step or two from the goal line with nobody around him, he raised the ball in celebration -- and dropped it. He managed to regain possession of the loose football, but when he did, he was standing on the end line. The ball was awarded to Western Kentucky on a touchback.

The Hilltoppers couldn't move. As the punting units took the field, Mark Richt was reluctant to use Henderson again -- but not because of his big gaffe. Henderson had injured a hamstring on the return. But the embarrassed youngster wanted to redeem himself, and he begged his head coach to let him return the kick. Richt relented.

BULLDOGS

Probably the only way Henderson could gain redemption from his teammates and the sellout crowd was to pull off the unlikely feat of returning the punt for a touchdown. Incredibly, that's what he did, taking the kick 67 yards. Georgia won easily 48-12.

Henderson got the chance to return more punts that season, finishing first in the SEC and fifth in the nation with a 14.7 average. He was named first-team All-SEC.

In our capitalistic society, we know all about redemption. Just think "rebate" or store or product coupons. To receive the rebates or the discount, though, we must redeem them, cash them in.

"Redemption" is a business term; it reconciles a debt, restoring one party to favor by making amends as was the case with Mikey Henderson and his second punt return. In the Bible, a slave could obtain his freedom only upon the paying of money by a redeemer. In other words, redemption involves the cancelling of a debt the individual cannot pay on his own.

While literal, physical slavery is incomprehensible to us today, we nevertheless live much like slaves in our relationship to sin. On our own, we cannot escape from its consequence, which is death. We need a redeemer, someone to pay the debt that gives us the forgiveness from sin we cannot give ourselves.

We have such a redeemer. He is Jesus Christ, who paid our debt not with money, but with his own blood.

I was holding that ball so tight, nobody could have taken it away from me.
-- Mikey Henderson on the punt return that redeemed him

**To accept Jesus Christ as your savior is to believe
that his death was a selfless act of redemption.**

DAY 65

A ROARING SUCCESS

Read Galatians 5:16-26.

*"So I say, live by the Spirit. . . . The sinful nature desires
what is contrary to the Spirit. . . . I warn you, as I did
before, that those who live like this will not inherit the
kingdom of God" (vv. 16, 17, 21).*

Lynn Hughes was so successful on defense in 1966 for the
league champions that he was first-team All-SEC at safety. For the
team, though, his greatest success may have been at quarterback.

Hughes played quarterback for Vince Dooley's first team, in
1964. With the arrival of Preston Ridlehuber and Kirby Moore in
1965, he was moved over to defense. He thrived there, leading the
SEC in interceptions and being named First-Team All-SEC.

In the 1966 Kentucky game with Georgia trailing 15-14, Moore
suffered an ankle injury late in the third quarter. Dooley made an
unusual decision; he passed on backup Rick Arrington, who had
played in each of Georgia's first five games, and told Hughes to
step across the line.

Hughes responded by leading the offense on a 7-play, 53-yard
drive that he topped off with a 10-yard scoring run. Dooley decided
to go for two, and running back Kent Lawrence rushed onto the
field with the play the head coach wanted written on a sheet of
paper. Hughes passed to Sandy Johnson for the two points, and a
22-15 Bulldog lead. Later in the same quarter, Hughes drove the
offense downfield for a Bobby Etter field goal.

BULLDOGS

Georgia won 27-15 with Hughes rushing and passing for 59 yards, which doesn't sound too awfully successful except for the fact that the senior hadn't played quarterback since the Kentucky game of the year before. He hadn't even practiced at the position.

"You'd never know he'd been on the defensive unit," Dooley said, "for he grabbed the controls in spectacular fashion." And, considering the comeback win, successful fashion also.

Are you a successful person? Your answer, of course, depends upon how you define success. Is the measure of your success based on the number of digits in your bank balance, the square footage of your house, that title on your office door, the size of your boat?

Certainly the world determines success by wealth, fame, prestige, awards, and possessions. Our culture screams that life is all about gratifying your own needs and wants. If it feels good, do it. It's basically the Beach Boys' philosophy of life.

But all success of this type has one glaring shortcoming: You can't take it with you. Eventually, Daddy takes the T-bird away. Like life itself, all these things are fleeting.

A more lasting way to approach success is through the spiritual rather than the physical. The goal becomes not money or backslaps by sycophants but eternal life spent with God. Success of that kind is forever.

If you coach for 25 years and never win a championship but you influence three people for Christ, that is success.
> *-- Oklahoma women's basketball coach Sherri Coale*

**Success isn't permanent, and failure isn't fatal --
unless it's in your relationship with God.**

DAY 66

PROVE IT!

Read Matthew 3.

"But John tried to deter him, saying, 'I need to be baptized by you, and do you come to me?'" (v. 14)

He was so slow and so small that even Vanderbilt wouldn't let him walk on. So he proved himself in spectacular fashion, including a legendary Bulldog play.

Simply put, Nate Taylor did not possess the physical attributes necessary to be a football player in the SEC. "He couldn't run fast," said UGA linebackers coach Chip Wisdom. "I don't think Nate ever broke five-flat" in the 40-yard "dash." Standing only 5'10" and weighing only 193 pounds, Taylor also wasn't really big enough to be a successful major-college linebacker.

He wasn't recruited out of high school. After Vanderbilt turned down his request to walk on in 1979, he went to Athens -- where he really had to prove himself -- and walked on. Relegated to the scout team that practiced against the varsity, the first coach he caught the attention of was offensive line coach Wayne McDuffie -- because he was consistently making the linemen look bad.

Against South Carolina in the third game of the '79 season, Taylor proved himself beyond a doubt. The Dawgs suddenly found themselves short of linebackers. "I couldn't find anybody else to put in the game," Wisdom said. Taylor "wasn't supposed to be playing, but I ran him in." He made 18 tackles, received a scholarship the following week, and started every game the rest of his career. He led the team in tackles in both 1979 and 1980.

Taylor is most remembered for his hit that caused a fumble recovered by Pat McShea at the Georgia 5 in the closing minutes of the season opener in 1980. The play saved the 16-15 win over Tennessee and was elevated to legendary status when the Dawgs went on to win the national title.

Like Nate Taylor, you, too, have to prove yourself over and over again in your life. To your teachers, to that guy you'd like to date, to your parents, to your bosses, to the loan officer. It's always the same question: "Am I good enough?" Practically everything we do in life is aimed at proving that we are.

And yet, when it comes down to the most crucial situation in our lives, the answer is always a decisive and resounding "No!" Are we good enough to measure up to God? To deserve our salvation? John the Baptist knew he wasn't, and he was not only Jesus' relative but God's hand-chosen prophet. If he wasn't good enough, what chance do we have?

The notion that only "good" people can be church members is a perversion of Jesus' entire ministry. Nobody is good enough – without Jesus. Everybody is good enough – with Jesus. That's not because of anything we have done for God, but because of what he has done for us. We have nothing to prove to God.

How does this guy do that? You don't know how. You just know he does, so you play him.
-- Linebackers coach Chip Wisdom on Nate Taylor

The bad news is we can't prove to God's
satisfaction how good we are; the good news
is that because of Jesus we don't have to.

SIZE MATTERS

Read Luke 19:1-10.

"[Zacchaeus] wanted to see who Jesus was, but being a short man he could not, because of the crowd. So he ran ahead and climbed a sycamore-fig tree to see him" (vv. 3-4).

In college football, size really does matter. Except perhaps in the case of Bulldog center David Andrews.

When the UGA offensive line gathered in the fall of 2012, head coach Mark Richt said Andrews was easy to spot because he was -- shorter than everybody else. It's not that Andrews was THAT short. After all, he stands 6-foot-2. His weight at Georgia was officially listed at 295 pounds his sophomore season. Thus, he is taller and heavier than about 90 percent of the general U.S. population.

But clearly, Andrews is shorter than the average starting center of a major college football team. The man he replaced, four-year starter Ben Jones, was 20 pounds heavier and two inches taller.

The coaches were very much aware of their center's height, or the lack of it. Offensive line coach Will Friend and offensive coordinator Mike Bobo were known to join some of the players in cracking short jokes at Andrews' expense. He admitted that for a while the heckling got under his skin. "It used to tick me off," he said. But, "it just kind of fuels you to work harder."

And that work yielded results. Despite battling defensive linemen heavier and taller than he, Andrews played in ten games as a freshman in 2011 and then started every game in 2012.

That success resulted from a major change Andrews had to make in the way he approached his position. In high school at his small private school, his size allowed him to overpower opponents. At Georgia, he had to work at using his lack of size to his advantage, which meant proper technique on every play.

"Everyone talks about size and stuff," Andrews said, but what matters "is the size of the fight in the dog." And this Dog, no matter his size, has plenty of fight in him.

Bigger is better! Such is one of the most powerful mantras of our time. We expand our football stadiums. We augment our body parts surgically. Hey, make that a triple cheeseburger and a large order of fries! My company is bigger than your company. Even our church buildings must be bigger to be better. About the only exception to our all-consuming drive for bigness is our waistlines.

But size obviously didn't matter to Jesus. After all, salvation came to the house of an evil tax collector who was so short he had to climb a tree to catch a glimpse of Jesus. Zacchaeus indeed had a big bank account; he was a big man in town even if his own people scorned him. But none of that – including Zacchaeus' height – mattered; Zacchaeus received salvation because of his repentance, which revealed itself in a changed life.

The same is true for us today. What matters is the size of the heart devoted to our Lord.

There's nothing I can do about it. It's what God blessed me with.
-- David Andrews on his height

Size matters to Jesus, but only the size
of the heart of the one who would follow him.

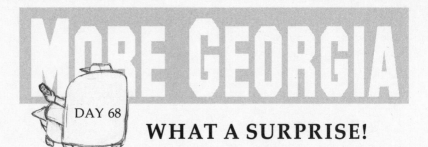

DAY 68

WHAT A SURPRISE!

Read 1 Thessalonians 5:1-11.

"But you, brothers, are not in darkness so that this day should surprise you like a thief" (v. 4).

The Gator head coach's decision was such a surprise that it surprised his own players. The result was a piece of Bulldog lore.

The Dawgs of 1975 were a nice 6-2 when they flew down to Jacksonville for the annual showdown with the Florida Gators. Still, they weren't expected to give Florida too much of a fight because that particular Gator squad was generally "regarded as perhaps the best team ever at Florida."

Nevertheless, the Dawgs stood toe-to-toe with the Gators and slugged it out. Late in the game, the Red and Black had managed only a 21-yard field goal from Allan Leavitt, but the Dog defense had hung grimly on all day, holding the powerful Gator offense to a lone touchdown and a 7-3 lead.

Then from its own 20 with 3:42 to play, Georgia pulled off one of the most famous plays in school history. Quarterback Matt Robinson pitched to Richard Appleby on what looked like the tight end around the Dogs had run several times before. This time, though, Appleby planted his feet and sailed the ball as far as he could. Forty-five yards away flanker Gene Washington trotted all by his lonesome. UGA suddenly led the surprised Gators 10-7.

Florida desperately tried to save itself, driving to a first down at the Georgia 21. The Dawg defense had one more stop in it, forcing a fourth and 10 with 50 seconds left. That's when the Gator head coach pulled his surprise. With everyone on his sideline expecting the team to go for it in an effort to win the school's first-ever SEC title, the head coach called for a field goal.

Caught by surprise, the Gator snapper had not warmed up. The snap was poor, the kicker's timing was thrown off, and the kick never got off the ground. Georgia had surprised the country.

Surprise birthday parties are a delight. And what's the fun of opening Christmas presents when we already know what's in them? Some surprises in life provide us with experiences that are both joyful and delightful.

Generally, though, we expend energy and resources to avoid most surprises and the impact they may have upon our lives. We may be surprised by the exact timing of a baby's arrival, but we nevertheless have the bags packed beforehand and the nursery all set for its occupant. Paul used this very image (v. 3) to describe the Day of the Lord, when Jesus will return to claim his own and establish his kingdom. We may be caught by surprise, but we must still be ready.

The consequences of being caught unprepared by a baby's insistence on being born are serious indeed. They pale, however, beside the eternal effects of not being ready when Jesus returns. We prepare ourselves just as Paul told us to (v. 8): We live in faith, hope, and love, ever on the alert for that great, promised day.

Surprise me.
-- Yogi Berra to his wife on where she should bury him

**The timing of Jesus' return will be a surprise;
the consequences should not be.**

DAY 69

TIME FOR A CHANGE

Read Romans 6:1-14.

"Just as Christ was raised from the dead through the glory of the Father, we too may live a new life" (v. 4).

Lizzy Stemke hadn't gotten over one life-changing event when the call came for another.

On Dec. 22, 2010, Stemke was hired as the sixth head coach in the history of the Bulldog volleyball program. The whole process was a bit unusual. For instance, she didn't come to Athens for her interview; instead, the entire search committee, including athletic director Greg McGarity, flew to Nebraska to meet with her. Also, her husband made the trip to Athens to check out The Classic City for her.

Why such an unusual scenario? Only two weeks before she was hired by Georgia, Stemke had given birth to her daughter. She really hadn't planned for two such life-changing events to happen right on top of each other, but she didn't really mind.

"To me, one big life event plus another equals perfect timing," she said. "You can't always control timing. I wasn't necessarily searching to leave Nebraska, especially with having a baby on the way." But UGA was definitely interested in having her leave Nebraska, where she had been an assistant coach for four seasons after a pair of years as an assistant at North Carolina.

Because of her pregnancy, though, Stemke couldn't make the long trip to Athens. So the search committee went to her about ten days after her daughter's birth. She still couldn't travel when the time came for her to visit the campus. Her husband, Kevin, a Ray Guy Award winner at Wisconsin as the best college punter in the country, made the trip to scout Athens out.

While moving halfway across the country was a big change, Stemke wasn't exactly unfamiliar with the SEC. She grew up in New Orleans; one brother played basketball at Ole Miss, another baseball at Tennessee, and a sister played volleyball at Florida. She changed her family's pattern by playing volleyball at Wisconsin.

Anyone who asserts no change is needed in his or her life just isn't paying attention. Every life has doubt, worry, fear, failure, frustration, unfulfilled dreams, and unsuccessful relationships in some combination. The memory and consequences of our past often haunt and trouble us.

Simply recognizing the need for change in our lives, though, doesn't mean the changes that will bring about hope, joy, peace, and fulfillment will occur. We need some power greater than ourselves or we wouldn't be where we are.

So where can we turn to? Where lies the hope for a changed life? It lies in an encounter with the Lord of all Hope: Jesus Christ. For a life turned over to Jesus, change is inevitable. With Jesus in charge, the old self with its painful and destructive ways of thinking, feeling, loving, and living is transformed.

A changed life is always only a talk with Jesus away.

Let's do it all at once.
-- Lizzy Stemke on her two major changes in December 2010

**In Jesus lie the hope and the power
that change lives.**

DAY 70

DOOR PRIZE

Read Acts 16:6-15.

"Paul and his companions traveled . . ., having been kept by the Holy Spirit from preaching the word in the province of Asia" (v. 6).

Because David Pollack trusted God, when a door slammed in his face, he expected another to be opened.

From 2002-04, Pollack won two Hendricks Awards as the best defensive end in the nation, two SEC Defensive Player of the Year awards, a Lombardi Award as college football's best lineman, and a Bednarik Award as the country's best defensive player.

His future seemed set, especially when the Cincinnati Bengals took him 17th overall in the 2005 NFL draft. What was expected to be a storied pro career, though, lasted sixteen games. "If you blinked, you would have missed it," Pollack said.

In the second game of his second NFL season, Pollack broke his neck making a tackle. He suffered no paralysis but underwent surgery and wore a neck brace for months. "He never played another snap again of the game he loved," the game that had been his obsession since he was 6 years old. He officially retired in 2008.

So that slamming door left Pollack bewildered, disappointed, angry, and confused, right? Not at all. His strong faith in God kept him grounded throughout his life-changing ordeal. Because of his absolute faith in God, "he was emotionally well-equipped to carry on," to look for the door he expected God to open for him.

BULLDOGS

"I never said or thought, 'Why me?'" Pollack said. "Getting hurt just happened." In fact, once he completed his rehab and was up and at 'em again, he came to regard the injury as a blessing. "I would have beat my body for the next 10, 12, 15 years," he said. "I would have been one of those guys who can barely walk and has a lot of broken fingers and other health issues."

Instead, he found that door God opened for him, starting a radio-TV broadcasting career and even landing his own show on ESPN. "I feel incredibly blessed to have what I have," Pollack said.

A rather benign aspect of our daily lives, a door is one of the most powerful metaphors we have for our spiritual lives. As David Pollack did with football and as Paul did with his inability to preach the Gospel in Asia, we often find the door to one path in our lives closed. That's often confusing and disappointing to us because we can't see in the short run what God has for us for eternity. We must, therefore, trust in God, convicted in our faith that when he closes one door, he opens another.

The door is a metaphor also for the most important moment in our lives. The Bible provides us the image of Jesus standing at the door of our hearts and knocking like a polite and unassuming guest. He'll step inside only when, or if, we open the door and invite him in. Our initial decision to open the door of our hearts for Jesus thus allows us to follow God's will for our lives by perceiving and then stepping through the doors he opens for us.

God never closes one door without opening another one.
-- David Pollack

When we open the door of our hearts to Jesus,
God opens doors in our lives.

DAY 71

POP THE QUESTION

Read Matthew 16:13-17.

"'But what about you?' he asked. 'Who do you say I am?'" (v. 15)

Joe Burson had a question for one of the coaches at halftime. He must have listened studiously to the answer because he acted on it with an exciting play that was key in a huge Bulldog upset.

1962 was not kind to UGA football. Wally Butts had resigned on Dec. 23, 1960, after 22 seasons as the head Dawg. The job went to Johnny Griffith, UGA's freshman coach and a halfback on the undefeated 1946 team. His first team went 3-7, and the '62 team was only 2-3-3 when it went to Auburn. The Tigers were 6-1 and in the hunt for the SEC title.

As one writer put it, "In 1962, the Bulldogs' running game was nearly nonexistent, perhaps the worst in Georgia history." Thus, the Dogs rode the talented arm of quarterback Larry Rakestraw. He found halfback Don Porterfield for a first-half TD, but Auburn led 14-7 at the break.

In the locker room at halftime, sophomore cornerback Joe Burson popped a question to assistant coach Bobby Proctor. He asked if he could gamble and go for an interception since the Auburn quarterback had thrown to Burson's short man in the first half. Proctor said he could but had a warning: "Don't you dare try it unless you're sure you can intercept."

Rakestraw and Porterfield teamed up to surprise Auburn

again in the last half and tied the game at 14. In the fourth quarter, Bill McCullough booted a 48-yard field goal, the second-longest in school history at the time, and Georgia led 17-14.

All the while, Burson considered the answer to his question and waited. With 8:21 to play, he gambled on the interception, got it, and sped 87 yards for a touchdown.

Auburn never recovered, and Georgia grabbed a 30-21 upset.

Life is an ongoing search for answers, and thus whether our life is lived richly or is wasted is largely determined by both the quality and the quantity of the answers we find. Life is indeed one question after another. What's for dinner? Can we afford a new car? What kind of team will Georgia have this season?

But we also continuously seek answers to questions at another, more crucial level. What will I do with my life? Why am I here? Why does God allow suffering and tragedy?

An aspect of wisdom is reconciling ourselves to and being comfortable with the fact that we will never know all of the answers. Equally wise is the realization that the answers to many of life's more momentous questions lie within us, not beyond us.

The question that Jesus asked Peter overrides all others: "Who do you say I am?" Peter gave the one and only correct answer: "You are the Son of the Living God." How you answer that question is really the only one that matters, since it decides not just how you spend your life but how you spend eternity.

If you miss that ball, it'll be an Auburn touchdown.
-- Bobby Proctor with a caution in answering Joe Burson at halftime

**Only one question in life determines
your eternal fate: Whom do you say Jesus is?**

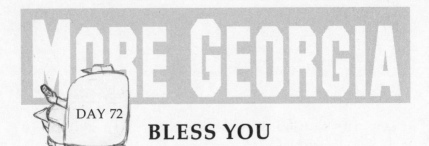

DAY 72

BLESS YOU

Read Romans 5:1-11.

*"We also rejoice in our sufferings because we know that
suffering produces perseverance; perseverance, character;
and character, hope. And hope does not disappoint us"
(vv. 3-5a).*

Having to stop and fill up with gas is just one of life's little nui-
sances, but in one case, that inconvenience turned into one of the
UGA football program's greatest blessings.

In the summer of 1939, Bill Hartman, the backfield coach for
Wally Butts, took a recruiting trip to Ohio. Back then, the drive
took a day and a half, and nothing about the trip went well for
the legendary Bulldog coach. He went to Youngstown to put
the Bulldog rush on, as he put it, "the best back in Ohio." When
Hartman arrived, though, he learned the boy had already decided
to play for Ohio State, which he subsequently did.

His long trip apparently a waste of time, Hartman stopped on
his way out of town to fill up for the return drive to Athens. He
struck up a conversation with the station attendant, who told him,
"The best back in the state really lives right down the street here."

Hartman turned his Plymouth around and drove right down
that street to find the player's father on the front porch. Many
words later, the coach had an agreement from the player that he
would take a recruiting visit to Athens.

That player was Frank Sinkwich, who is, of course, a Bulldog

BULLDOGS

and a college football legend, the first player from the South to win the Heisman Trophy (1942). He was also the AP Male Athlete of the Year in '42 and a two-time All-America. He was inducted into the College Football Hall of Fame in 1954.

Before he agreed to play for Georgia, however, Sinkwich had a condition: The Dogs had to offer a scholarship to his buddy. The coaches didn't hesitate. That buddy was George Poschner, an All-American end in 1942.

Who ever knew that filling up with gasoline could ultimately provide such blessings for the Dawgs?

We just never know what God is up to. We can know, though, that he's always busy preparing blessings for us and that if we trust and obey him, he will pour out those blessings upon us.

Some of those blessings, however, often come to us disguised as was the case with Bill Hartman's trip to Ohio. Quite frequently, only after we can look back upon what we have endured or undergone do we come to appreciate it as a blessing.

The key lies in trusting God, in realizing that God isn't out to destroy us but instead is interested only in doing good for us, even if that means allowing us to endure the consequences of a difficult lesson. God doesn't manage a candy store; more often, he relates to us as a stern but always loving father. If we truly love and trust God, no matter what our situation is now, he has blessings in store for us. This, above all, is our greatest hope.

Always have the attitude of gratitude and count your blessings.
-- Former NFL head coach Tony Dungy

Life's hardships are often transformed into blessings when we endure them trusting in God.

DAY 73

CHILD'S PLAY

Read James 1:19-27.

"Religion that God our Father accepts as pure and faultless is this: to look after orphans and widows in their distress and to keep oneself from being polluted by the world" (v. 27).

Mark and Katharyn Richt's family is a living witness to their commitment to the Bible's admonition to care for the orphans.

In late 1998, the Richts were already the parents of two boys, Jon and David, when a Sunday school message about caring for the widows and the orphans resonated with them. "While our sons, Jonathan and David, have been definite blessings, we felt like there was more of us to give," Katharyn said. "What are we doing to help?" Mark asked himself.

About the same time, Katharyn's sister-in-law visited an orphanage in the Ukraine and taped her journey. The Richts watched the tape and first saw Anya, a tiny blond with a facial deformity. Mark recalled asking himself if anyone would adopt this child. "I was thinking, probably not, so maybe we should," he said.

In July 1999, Katharyn traveled to the orphanage. "Anya was so small and vulnerable and tiny," she said of the 30-month-old child who weighed only eighteen pounds. But she also met and was captivated by Ruslan, who now is called Zach. He "was abandoned and left in a drawer," she said. "I'm not even sure at what age or how long."

BULLDOGS

Mark soon joined Katharyn overseas. After much discussion and prayer, they decided to adopt both children. "I am thankful that the Lord has allowed Mark and me to be the parents to help Anya and Zach to grow up," Katharyn said in 2009. "We have undoubtedly gained more than they have."

As was the case with Anya and Zach in the Ukraine, childhood is often not the idyllic time we imagine it to be for the world's youngsters. That's because an imbalance of power is at the heart of the parent-child relationship and the ones wielding the power frequently abuse it.

In his role as the creator of all life, God is in a sense the father of us all. Jesus, however, added a new layer of meaning to the traditional understanding of our relationship with God that truly renders us his children. Since only Christ is God's true son, only through Christ's mediation for us with God can the parent-child relationship be our own.

Our vision of a perfect childhood includes growth in a warm, safe, loving environment wherein the parent cherishes, protects, nurtures, and teaches the child. Love both restrains and guides the parent's power.

In other words, our conception of a perfect childhood matches God's vision for our relationship with him through Jesus.

You can't just talk about wanting to save the children. You have to do your part, and [adopting Anya and Zach] was our part.
-- Katharyn Richt

The physical act of birth renders us a child of our parents; the spiritual act of receiving Jesus Christ as our Lord renders us a child of God.

DAY 74

WORK ETHIC

Read Matthew 9:35-38.

"Then he said to his disciples, 'The harvest is plentiful but the workers are few. Ask the Lord of the harvest, therefore, to send out workers into his harvest field'" (vv. 37-38).

How in the world could a walk-on who was not recruited by any big-time school wind up playing the most minutes of anybody else on the Bulldog basketball team? Hard work had a lot to do with it.

At Parkview, Ricky McPhee was first-team All-Region and first-team All-Gwinnett County -- and no one really noticed. "I was under the radar recruiting-wise," he said. Only Gardner-Webb in North Carolina offered him a scholarship, and he took it.

After two seasons, though, McPhee craved a bigger program with better competition, so he walked on at Georgia. He sat out the 2007-08 season and played sparingly in 2008-09.

When Mark Fox arrived in April 2009, he liked what he saw in the senior who could flat hit a three-point shot. Also, as Fox said, "He's a guy who outworked probably several people rated ahead of him." "My mind-set coming in," McPhee said, "was to work as hard as I could on the practice floor and try to earn some respect."

That hard work paid off when McPhee's time came with the 2009-10 season. Fox first put him on scholarship and then into the starting lineup where McPhee stayed, minute after minute, game after game. He played more minutes than anybody else on the

BULLDOGS

team, including first-team All-SEC forward Trey Thompkins and guard Travis Leslie, both of whom would eventually be drafted by the NBA in the second round. McPhee averaged 9.6 points per game and was the team's third leading scorer.

And he earned that respect he sought. "We call him 'McThree,'" Thompkins said. "He's the one guy who holds our team together."

"It's crazy how things worked out," McPhee said, who admitted that he walked around campus smiling all the time. "I never thought in a million years I'd have a chance to start at UGA and be a contributor on the court and be a major minutes guy."

But he worked his way into every one of those major minutes.

Do you embrace hard work or try to avoid it? No matter how hard you may try, you really can't escape hard work. Funny thing about all these labor-saving devices like cell phones and laptop computers: You're working longer and harder than ever. For many of us, our work defines us perhaps more than any other aspect of our lives. But there's a workforce you're a part of that doesn't show up in any Labor Department statistics or any IRS records.

You're part of God's staff; God has a specific job that only you can do for him. It's often referred to as a "calling," but it amounts to your serving God where there is a need in the way that best suits your God-given abilities and talents

You should stand ready to work for God all the time, 24-7. Those are awful hours, but the benefits are out of this world.

I think he's the hardest worker on our team by far.
-- Bulldog center Albert Jackson on Ricky McPhee

God calls you to use the talents and gifts
he gave you to work for him.

DAY 75

JUST PERFECT

Read Matthew 5:43-48.

"Be perfect, therefore, as your heavenly Father is perfect"
(v. 48).

After Georgia scored one touchdown on a busted play, Chris
Conley finished Nebraska off with a reception on a record-setting
play the Dawgs ran to perfection.

In the 2013 Capital One Bowl, Georgia scored its most points
ever in a bowl game, winning 45-31 behind quarterback Aaron
Murray's record-setting five touchdown passes. After a 49-yard
Conley touchdown catch and the two-point conversion tied the
game at 31 late in the third quarter, the Dawgs grabbed the lead
for good on the first play of the fourth period. At the Husker 24,
Murray slipped to his right and sailed one toward tailback Keith
Marshall. He spun around and adjusted to the ball to haul it in
at the 3 and score. "He just threw a great ball and I reacted to it,"
Marshall said. "It was kind of a busted play."

There was nothing busted about the Bulldogs' final touchdown
of the day, the longest scoring play in UGA bowl history. Again,
Conley, a sophomore wide receiver, was Murray's target.

Conley is something of a Renaissance man. He sings and plays
the guitar and can pick out any tune on the piano after hearing
a note or two. He also writes poetry and songs and likes to draw.

What the Dawgs drew up with 11:03 left was a perfect play
that wrapped up the game. On third and long from the UGA 13,

BULLDOGS

offensive coordinator Mike Bobo guessed Nebraska would come with an all-out blitz. They did and he had the perfect call.

Tight end Arthur Lynch laid a perfect block on the defender who was assigned to Conley. The offensive line also executed perfectly across the front. "A pass receiver could not have been more open. As soon as Murray delivered the ball," everyone could see the perfectly executed play was an 87-yard touchdown.

Nobody's perfect; we all make mistakes every day. We botch our personal relationships; at work we seek competence and not perfection. To insist upon personal or professional perfection in our lives is to establish an impossibly high standard that will eventually destroy us physically, emotionally, and mentally.

Yet that is exactly the standard God sets for us. Our love is to be perfect, never ceasing, never failing, never qualified – just the way God loves us. And Jesus didn't limit his command to only preachers and goody-two-shoes types. All of his disciples are to be perfect as they navigate their way through the world's ambiguous definition and understanding of love.

But that's impossible! Well, not necessarily, if to love perfectly is to serve God wholeheartedly and to follow Jesus with single-minded devotion. Anyhow, in his perfect love for us, God makes allowance for our imperfect love and the consequences of it in the perfection of Jesus.

It was either going to be a huge play or a bust.
-- Aaron Murray on his 87-yard touchdown pass

In his perfect love for us, God provides a way
for us to escape the consequences
of our imperfect love for him: Jesus.

FAIL-SAFE

Read Luke 22:54-62.

"Peter remembered the word the Lord had spoken to him: 'Before the rooster crows today, you will disown me three times.' And he went outside and wept bitterly" (vv. 61b-62).

With the game tied when they came to bat in the bottom of the sixth, the Dogs loaded the bases and then didn't even get the ball out of the infield. So they failed. Or not.

Against Auburn on May 4, 2012, the teams locked into a 1-1 tie heading into the bottom of the sixth. Third baseman Curt Powell singled to drive senior first baseman Colby May home in the third inning, but that was about all the offense the Dogs had mustered. Meanwhile, sophomore lefthander Alex Wood, whose 2.73 ERA for the season was the best by a UGA starter since Dave Fleming's 2.08 in 1989, kept the Tigers in check.

Junior shortstop Kyle Farmer, who the next day would deliver a two-out RBI single for a walk-off 6-5 win in 11 innings, started the sixth with a single. That turned out to be the only solid hit the Dawgs could manage, but that failure didn't keep them from busting the game wide open.

The Bulldogs simply didn't need to hit the ball hard. They got all the help they needed from Auburn's generous pitchers, who suddenly developed some severe control problems. After a pair of walks loaded the bases, freshman Justin Bryan and sophomore outfielder Conor Welton each notched an RBI with a walk.

The Dawgs were handed another gift run when senior Peter Verdin, who finished up as sixth all-time in career stolen bases with 47, was hit by a pitch. Senior second baseman Levi Hyams, who led the team in hitting as a junior at .332, then actually did hit the ball. His groundout chased the fourth run of the inning home. Georgia led 5-1 after failing four times to get a hit with the bases loaded. The Dogs eventually won 5-2.

"Auburn helped us," UGA head coach David Perno admitted. "I don't care how it comes." In baseball, a big inning is a big inning even if you fail at the plate.

In life, failure is relative, usually defined by expectations and not necessarily by results For instance, a Bulldog baseball player who hits .300 is a star, but he fails seventy percent of the time.

And we are often our own harshest critics, beating ourselves up for our failings because we expected better. Never mind that our expectations were unrealistic to begin with.

The bad news about life is that failure – unlike success -- is inevitable. Only one man walked this earth perfectly and we're not him. The good news about life, however, is that failure isn't permanent. In life, we always have time to reverse our failures as did Peter, he who failed our Lord so abjectly.

The same cannot be said of death. In death we eternally suffer the consequences of our failure to follow that one perfect man.

We didn't get any hits, but guys had really good at-bats.
-- Curt Powell on the Dawgs' failure and success in the sixth inning

Only one failure in life dooms us to eternal failure in death: failing to follow Jesus Christ.

SWEET WORDS

Read Romans 8:28-39.
"In all these things we are more than conquerors through him who loved us" (v. 37).

Tommy Lawhorne was so overwhelmed that he admitted he was "scared to death." Then he got a little affirmation from his coach that settled him down -- even though he knew the man was lying to him.

In the long and storied history of UGA football, Lawhorne stands alone in that he started for three seasons at linebacker (1965-67) AND was the valedictorian of his graduating class. He arrived in Athens in the fall of 1964. Committed to his dream of medical school, he struggled that first quarter trying to balance a heavy academic load and football. "I kept plugging along," he said, making A+'s and serving as fodder for the varsity as a freshman wingback.

Shortly before the '65 opener against Alabama, a starting linebacker was injured. The coaches looked around and decided on Lawhorne. He scrimmaged the Saturday before the game, and "I had a pretty good day." He was not prepared, though, for what came next. The coaches named him a starter against the Tide.

"I was scared to death," Lawhorne said, which illustrated just how smart he was. He had practiced at linebacker for less than two weeks, and he was to take on the defending national champions. But the ultimate motivator, defensive coordinator Erk

BULLDOGS

Russell, was ready with some affirmation for his rookie. Chewing on his omnipresent cigar, Russell put his arm around Lawhorne's shoulder and declared, "I don't know of anybody in the world I would rather have starting for me than you."

The coach was lying and Lawhorne knew it, but that didn't change anything. "I was really jacked up to play," he said. He went out and helped the Dawgs stun the Tide 18-17.

You make a key decision. All excited, you tell your best friend or spouse and anxiously await a reaction. "Boy, that was dumb" is what you get. Or a friend's life spirals out of control into a total disaster. Do you pretend you don't know that messed-up person?

Everybody needs affirmation in some degree. That is, we all occasionally need someone to say something positive about us, that we are worth something, and that God loves us.

The follower of Jesus does what our Lord did when he encountered someone whose life was a mess. Rather than seeing what they were, he saw what they could become. Life is hard; it breaks us all to some degree. To be like Jesus, we see past the problems of the broken and the hurting and envision their potential, understanding that not condemning is not condoning.

The Christian's words of affirmation are the greatest, most joyous of all. They constitute a message of victory and triumph from which nothing can separate us or defeat us.

If my grandmother had been wearing an Alabama helmet I would have said, 'Look out, Granny, here it comes.'
*   -- Tommy Lawhorne about the '65 Alabama game*

**The greatest way to affirm lost persons
is to lead them to Christ.**

DAY 78

THE CHALLENGE

Read Matthew 4:12-25.

"Come, follow me," Jesus said (v. 19).

An unimpressed former Bulldog player challenged the Dawgs' manhood -- and Alabama paid the price.

The Bulldogs of 2002 were 4-0, but looming directly ahead on the horizon in Tuscaloosa was the Crimson Tide. Pat Dye didn't think Georgia was up to the challenge.

Dye was an All-American guard at Georgia in 1959 and 1960 who was an assistant coach for Bear Bryant at Alabama before serving as head coach and athletic director at Auburn. The week of the Georgia-Alabama game of Oct. 5, 2002, he appeared on a syndicated radio show to declare he was not impressed with his former team. The Dogs had notched a pair of close wins over Clemson and South Carolina and had coasted in back-to-back breathers against Northwestern State of Lousiana and New Mexico State. "They haven't played a good football team yet," Dye declared. He said Alabama was going to line up and run the football and play good defense. Then Dye delivered the clincher: "I don't believe Georgia is man enough to beat that."

As writer Rob Suggs put it, "Questioning someone's manhood is the 'double-dog dare' of Southern football." Naturally, Dye's words became "verbal kudzu"; they were everywhere. But the Vegas oddsmakers agreed with him and made Bama the favorite.

Thus challenged, the Bulldogs responded. They came out and

played "smash-mouth, helmet-smacking, pad-rattling varsity ball like real country boys played," the kind of football that a woefully misguided Missouri player in 2012 would call "old-man football" right before Georgia went out and stomped his team by 21 points.

When the dust had cleared, Georgia had beaten Alabama 27-25 and was off and running to the SEC championship.

Like the UGA athletic teams every time they take the field or the court, we are challenged daily. Life is a testing ground; God intentionally set it up that way. If we are to grow in character, confidence, and perseverance, and if we are to make a difference in the world, we must meet challenges head-on. Few things in life are as boring and as destructive to our sense of self-worth as a job that doesn't offer any challenges.

Our faith life is the same way. The moment we answered Jesus' call to "Come, follow me," we took on the most difficult challenge we will ever face. We are called to be holy by walking in Jesus' footsteps in a world that seeks to render our Lord irrelevant and his influence negligible. The challenge Jesus places before us is to put our faith and our trust in him and not in ourselves or the transitory values of the secular world.

Daily walking in Jesus' footsteps is a challenge, but the path takes us all the way right up to the gates of Heaven – and then right on through.

If they come over and beat Alabama, then they can beat on their chests when they go back to Athens.
-- Pat Dye before the 2002 Alabama game

To accept Jesus as Lord is to joyfully take on the challenge of living a holy life in an unholy world.

DAY 79

LAUGH IT UP

Read Genesis 21:1-7.

"Sarah said, 'God has brought me laughter, and everyone who hears about this will laugh with me'" (v. 6).

Vince Dooley's talks to his team the day before a game were always serious until a player turned one into a comedy routine.

The day before the 1978 game with Georgia Tech, sophomore cornerback Greg Bell revealed to his teammates that he could do dead-on impressions, including one of his head football coach. The word spread quickly among the players.

Dooley was delayed doing television interviews on the field, so the players had a little extra time waiting for him in the field house. The head man always talked to his players the day before a game, using a big grease board to illustrate his key points. Bell noted that Dooley wrote the same thing on the board every time. "I had memorized the speech. We all had," he said.

Not surprisingly, the players coaxed Bell into doing a Dooley routine with that grease board. He first wrote "No Mistakes" on the board and followed that up by pronouncing "We don't need to make any mistakes" in a perfect Dooley. The players fell out, and Bell kept going until someone noticed the head Dawg was coming. Bell erased everything and scurried to his seat.

The unsuspecting head coach didn't stand a chance. Right on cue, he wrote "No Mistakes" right over where Bell had written it. When his first words were, "We don't need to make any mistakes," the players went berserk with laughter. Annoyed, Dooley snapped his head around and they quieted.

But only until he wrote point No. 2, again right over where Bell had written it. The room just fell apart. "Get control of yourselves!" Dooley shouted, but it was no good. By the time he got to point No. 3, he had completely lost control of the meeting. In frustration, he barked, "Y'all know what to do, and you better do it tomorrow." The meeting was over.

Stand-up comedians are successful because they find humor in the world, and it's often hard for us to do that. "Laughter is foolish," an acerbic Solomon wrote in Ecclesiastes 2:2, his angst overwhelming him because he couldn't find much if anything in his world to laugh at.

We know how he felt. When we take a good look around at this world we live in, can we really find much to laugh at? It seems everywhere we look we find not just godlessness but ongoing and pervasive tragedy and misery.

Well, we can recognize as Sarah did that in God's innumerable gifts lie irresistible laughter. The great gift that is Jesus provides us with more than enough reason to laugh, no matter our situation. Through God's grace in Jesus Christ, we can laugh at death, at Satan, at the very gates of hell, at the world's pain.

Because they are of this world, our tears will pass. Because it is of God, our laughter will remain – forever.

Everybody couldn't stop laughing and talking.
-- Vince Dooley on the team meeting hijacked by Greg Bell

Of the world, sorrow is temporary;
of God, laughter is forever.

DAY 80

FUSSBUDGETS

Read Philippians 2:12-18.

"Do everything without complaining or arguing, so that you may become blameless and pure" (vv. 14,15a).

Lamar "Racehorse" Davis started to complain but then thought better of it, which led to Georgia's landing a Hall-of-Fame player.

In 1939, Davis, a high school senior, was invited to play in an all-star basketball game in Atlanta, an invitation he has always considered a mistake. The participants were listed alphabetically, but his name was near the bottom of the list. When his turn came for equipment, game sponsors had run out of basketball shoes, so they simply handed him a pair of football shoes.

That's when the slighted Davis thought of complaining to his coach, but had some second thoughts. An all-star football game was also to be played, and he was getting what amounted to an all-expense-paid vacation in Atlanta. He hushed up.

When Georgia Tech's Bobby Dodd, one of the coaches, asked Davis what he could do, he replied, "Block," which was the only thing he could think of at the moment. So he entered the all-star game as a blocking back and, as he put it, "blocked nobody." He did return an interception for a touchdown, running "out of sheer fright," he said. UGA track coach Spec Towns was in the stands and offered him a football scholarship.

Though he was there on the sideline teaming with Larry Munson for the dramatic Buck-Belue-to-Lindsay-Scott pass in 1980,

BULLDOGS

Loran Smith argues a play Davis made in the 1941 Auburn game could be "the most dramatic touchdown play" in Georgia football history. In a scoreless game, Auburn punted out of bounds to the Bulldog 35 with three seconds on the clock. As the gun went off ending the game, Davis caught a pass from Frankie Sinkwich and outran Auburn's defenders for a 65-yard touchdown.

The 7-0 win, which sent UGA to the Orange Bowl, may never have happened had Lamar Davis complained about his shoes.

Our usual and immediate reaction when we are wronged is to complain. Fussing may be natural, but it isn't spiritual.

Paul urged us to do as Lamar Davis did -- stifle our complaints -- to demonstrate the depth of our faith. Well now, just how does that work? Complaining is brought on by our circumstances; it's aimed at something or somebody. But when we complain, we are in fact declaring our failure to perceive that God is in charge of the moment. To grumble and to whine is thus to take our eyes off God. Complaining is nothing more than a spiritually immature reaction to a temporarily bothersome situation.

The more faith-filled response to a situation that tempts us to complain is prayer. While it may not immediately resolve the problem of the moment, it nevertheless allows us to escape from the unpleasantness blameless before God. And that's never anything to complain about.

I thought about those three meals a day with a two weeks stay in the plush Henry W. Grady Hotel and kept my mouth shut.
-- Lamar 'Racehorse' Davis on why he didn't complain about his shoes

Complaining is an unfit response to a temporary situation best resolved eternally by prayer.

DAY 81

AGAINST THE WALL

Read Exodus 14:5-31.

"'The Lord will fight for you; you need only to be still" (v. 14).

Maho Kowase was getting the daylights beat out of her, and as she went so did UGA's hopes in the 2012 NCAA Tournament. With her back against the wall, she responded with a comeback her head coach described as "amazing."

A sophomore from Japan, Kowase "looked like the last person [who] would save the season for the Georgia women's tennis team" in the tournament's second round. The sixth-ranked Bulldogs were in deep trouble against 24th-ranked Clemson. With the match tied at 3, it came town to Kowase, who promptly fell so far behind that the Clemson players could be forgiven for mentally preparing themselves for the next round.

Kowase's opponent blasted her 6-0 in the first set and jumped out to a 5-2 lead in the second, needing only one game to eliminate the Dawgs. "She wasn't playing bad," head coach Jeff Wallace said of Kowase. "The other girl was just absolutely outplaying her."

With her back against the wall, Kowase rallied. She won five straight games to force a third and deciding set. When Kowase got within 5-4 in the second set, Wallace told her if she could win the next game, she would win the match. She did, blowing past the flummoxed Tiger across the net 6-1 in the third set.

"Just simply amazing," Kowase admitted about her comeback,

echoing Wallace's assessment. "I couldn't do anything, . . . but I just tried my best and waited for the chance."

So what did Kowase do to celebrate her comeback that bailed her team out and kept them alive? Call mama, of course. It was already Sunday morning back home in Japan -- Mother's Day.

Maybe it was circumstances beyond your control. Or perhaps it was a series of bad decisions you made in all honesty. Whatever the reasons, like Maho Kowase, you find yourself with your back against the wall. You have nowhere to run, you can't hide, and your friends – if they're still around – can't or won't help.

You don't have an army charging down upon you with your annihilation on its mind as the panic-stricken Israelites did, but today's world can accomplish your destruction without chariots and swords. Your enemies are much more subtle. Whether it's office politics, medical pros, or a collapsing home life -- you sometimes stand back against the wall and watch everyone else count you out.

What then? Is it all over?

The fight could just be starting – if you come to the realization that in such a situation, there is only one who is powerful enough to overcome your circumstances. Moses knew exactly what to do and so should you. That wall you're up against can begin to teeter and crumble in response to one powerful prayer: "O God, help me – because you are God."

She is such a fighter.

-- UGA coach Jeff Wallace on Maho Kowase

**When your back is against the wall,
team up with God and come out swinging.**

DAY 82

BEING DIFFERENT

Read Daniel 3.

*"We want you to know, O king, that we will not serve
your gods or worship the image of gold you have set up"
(v. 18).*

Ask Arthur Lynch about how his life was growing up, and he quite possibly will say that it was different.

Fellow tight end Aron White, whose Bulldog career ended in 2011, referred to Lynch as "the man," adding, "There's no other way I can put it." He wasn't referring only to Lynch's size. At 6′ 5″, 270 lbs., Lynch was hard to miss, the total package of the blocking and receiving tight end. White also had reference to Lynch's heart.

As a junior in 2012, Lynch emerged as a real threat in quarterback Aaron Murray's arsenal. He hauled in 24 passes for 431 yards, both fourth on the team. He scored three touchdowns, including one in the win over Nebraska in the Capital One Bowl.

The thought about Lynch's heart refers to his childhood in Dartmouth, Mass., and his determination to overcome some very serious obstacles in his life. "When we were younger we didn't exactly have the most," Lynch once said in discussing his past. "We always had clothes on our backs and food to eat but it wasn't the easiest to support four kids."

That's because when Lynch was 14, his dad left home. "Most of my earliest memories are just being with my mom or my grandfather," Lynch recalled. Lynch's face always brightens when he speaks of "Ma Dukes." "Seeing how strong she was really just made me a better person, and it made me realize how lucky I am to have her," he said. To honor his mom and his grandfather, he changed his last name to Lynch when he was 18.

The name change was just part of the somewhat different life Arthur Lynch had on his way to Athens and to being "the man." "It helped me become a man," he said about his childhood.

Each of us is different in some way, especially if we are Christians. That's because we serve a risen Christ who calls us to be different from the secular world around us, and therein lies the great conflict of the Christian life in contemporary America.

How many of us really consider that even in our secular society we struggle to conform? We are all geeks in a sense. We can never truly conform no matter how hard we try because we were not created by God to live in such a sin-filled world in the first place. Thus, when Christ calls us to be different by following and espousing Christian beliefs, principles, and practices, he is summoning us to the lifestyle we were born for.

The most important step in being different for Jesus is realizing and admitting what we really are: We are children of God; we are Christians. Only secondarily are we citizens of a secular world. That world both scorns and disdains us for being different; Jesus both praises and loves us for it.

My life would have been different if my dad was around, but I don't think it would have been different in a bad or good way.
-- Arthur Lynch on his childhood

The lifestyle Jesus calls us to is different from that of the world, but it is the way we were born to live.

DAY 83

WISE GUYS

Read James 3:13-18.

"Who is wise and understanding among you? Let him show it by his good life, by deeds done in the humility that comes from wisdom" (v. 13).

In their wisdom, Chick-fil-A bigwigs figured they had come up with a really great promotion to launch their sponsorship of a bowl game. Uh – no.

The Bulldogs were 8-3 in 1998 and ended the regular season ranked 19th in the nation. They accepted an invitation to play 12th-ranked Virginia in the Chick-fil-A Peach Bowl, the Atlanta-based outfit's first year of corporate sponsorship of the game.

To highlight the occasion, the company decided to give every spectator a miniature cow. They cost Chick-fil-A $300,000 and were hauled into the stadium in four tractor-trailers. A plush little black-and-white cow was placed in the cup holder of every seat.

It was true marketing genius -- until the second quarter and UVa scored after an interception. About 1,000 of the cows went airborne, sailing down onto the field. When UGA suffered three picks over five minutes, the cow deluge had begun. A message on the video board pleaded with spectators to stop throwing their cows. The immediate response was more airborne bovines.

The Dogs rallied from a 21-0 deficit with runs from Olandis Gary and quarterback Quincy Carter eventually propelling UGA to a 35-27 lead with 7:01 to play. The Cavs scored with 1:34 left and missed the two-point conversion. They then recovered an onside kick but missed a field goal with 19 seconds left. Immediately, "it appeared that any fan who had yet to toss his or her toy cow during the game flung it onto the field," Virginia fans in disgust, Dawg fans in celebration of the 35-33 win.

As the fiasco of the flying cows indicates, what often appears to be wisdom sometimes isn't. Wisdom is sort of like art; we can't really define it, but we know it when we encounter it. Unless Jesus is the one furnishing the definition.

The world finds its wisdom in places such as classrooms where teachers prowl, boardrooms where business leaders plan, and kitchens where moms patrol. Secular wisdom thus demonstrates itself in results or by achievements.

Jesus doesn't see wisdom in that way at all. Instead, true wisdom is demonstrated by a life filled with good deeds and with humility. A wise follower of Jesus is moral, considerate of others, and merciful. She loves peace, not strife, and her ambition is channeled down paths that help others.

The world ultimately sees wisdom as accumulating a bunch of things you leave behind when you die. Jesus views wisdom as living in a way that reaps a harvest of salvation and eternal life. Little wisdom is required to discern which view ultimately is wise and which is foolish.

On a night when cows flew, [Quincy Carter] became a leader of a triumphant Georgia team.
-- Writer Patrick Garbin

**Worldly wisdom results in death; Christly wisdom
results in eternal life. So which is truly wise?**

DAY 84

THE PIONEER SPIRIT

Read Luke 5:1-11.

"So they pulled their boats up on shore, left everything and followed him" (v. 11).

When UGA offensive coordinator Mike Bobo surprised Aaron Murray with a five-receiver formation during the 2012 season, the junior quarterback's reaction was typical. "I don't think anybody in Georgia history has ever seen that before," he said. Well, at least not since the 1950s.

That's when Wally Butts, a true pioneer in the collegiate passing game, was airing it out, just as he had since 1939 as the Bulldogs' head coach. Butts' basic football philosophy was at odds with the prevailing attitude of his day, which called for slugging it out with a power running game. Instead, more than six decades before college football became an air show, Butts had one in Athens.

It was entirely of his own making, since he was the pioneer and thus the expert. "He just liked passing and exciting offense," said Bill Hartman, a member of the College Football Hall of Fame who played for Georgia in the 1930s and later coached under Butts.

The coach "had an imaginative football mind, and he could fill up a yellow notepad with pass plays in a matter of minutes." "We were the first team to throw 35 passes in a game," Hartman recalled in an age when 35 passes amounted to half a season's attempts for most teams. The Dawgs frequently entered a game with more than one hundred different pass plays to pick from.

BULLDOGS

In the late 1950s, Butts was the only college coach in the country to use five-receiver sets. While most coaches still used the single wing, he moved to the T formation, which gave him the flexibility he needed to throw the ball.

Bulldog legend Charley Trippi, perhaps Butts' greatest player, said that when he got to the pros, "I could tell immediately that they didn't know half as much about the passing game as Coach Butts. He was way ahead of them." He was the pioneer.

Going to a place in your life you've never been before requires a willingness to take risks and face uncertainty head-on. You may have never helped change the way the game of football is played, but you've had your moments when your latent pioneer spirit manifested itself. That time you changed careers, ran a marathon, volunteered at a homeless shelter, learned Spanish, or went back to school.

While attempting new things invariably begets apprehension, the truth is that when life becomes too comfortable and too familiar, it gets boring. The same is true of God, who is downright dangerous because he calls us to be anything but comfortable as we serve him. He summons us to continuously blaze new trails in our faith life, to follow him no matter what. Stepping out on faith is risky all right, but the reward is a life of accomplishment, adventure, and joy that cannot be equaled anywhere else.

We had the west coast offense at Georgia in 1939.
-- Bill Hartman, 'the ultimate role model for all loyal UGA alumni'

**Unsafe and downright dangerous, God calls us
out of the place where we are comfortable to a life
of adventure and trailblazing in his name.**

DAY 85

AD MAN

Read Mark 1:21-28.

"News about him spread quickly over the whole region"
(v. 28).

Advertising may pay but it costs, too, except in the case of Mark Fox's basketball team -- thanks to a walk-on who had yet to play.

Connor Nolte, a 6'-7" forward from Alpharetta, played two seasons at Furman (2007-09) before transferring to Georgia. The rules required that he sit out the 2009-10 season, but they didn't keep him from making a significant contribution to the UGA program.

Nolte has a website called passersremorse.com. At the time, he posted a trick shot on the day of each UGA game. In February 2010, he talked head football coach Mark Richt into shooting a one-handed reverse free throw, which he posted. The trick shot garnered more than 38,000 views on YouTube.

But Nolte was just getting started. Later in the month, he posted "a crazy shot by Fox, who twice bounced the ball off the top of the shot clock and through the net from the stands." "Back-to back, jack," Fox crowed. ESPN picked up on the quite amazing feat, including it twice among its top 10 plays-of-the-day feature.

The UGA program couldn't have paid any amount of money for advertising that resulted in more exposure. "I woke up the other day and I had a million messages about ESPN," Fox said. "So, yeah, it's been amazing. . . . It's been great publicity."

The publicity only increased when roundball legend Charles

BULLDOGS

Barkley agreed to take part in a Nolte posting. As Barkley looked on approvingly, Nolte dunked without shoes. "He dunks in his socks. And that's why it rocks," Barkley said.

Nolte averaged ten minutes per game playing time and scored 40 points with 38 rebounds in 2010-11. As a senior in 2011-12, he averaged 6.5 minutes per game, scoring 30 points and grabbing 25 boards. None of his contributions on the court, though, had the effect on UGA basketball that all that free publicity did.

Commercials and advertisements for products, goods, and services inundate us. Watch NASCAR: Decals cover the cars and the drivers' uniforms. Turn on your computer: Ads pop up. TV, radio, newspapers, billboards, every square inch of every wall -- everyone's one trying to get the word out the best way possible.

Jesus was no different in that he used the most effective and efficient means of advertising he had at his disposal to spread his message of salvation and hope among the masses. That was word of mouth.

In his ministry, Jesus didn't isolate himself; instead, he moved from town to town among the common folks, preaching, teaching, and healing. Those who encountered Jesus then told others about their experience, thus spreading the news about the good news. Almost two millennia later, nothing's really changed. Speaking to someone else about Jesus still remains the best way to get the word out, and the best advertisement of all is a changed life.

This kid got us into 10 million homes.

-- *Mark Fox on Connor Nolte*

The best advertising for Jesus is word of mouth, telling others what he has done for you.

DAY 86

TO TELL THE TRUTH

Read Matthew 5:33-37.

"Simply let your 'Yes' be 'Yes,' and your 'No,' 'No';
anything beyond this comes from the evil one" (v. 37).

One rather far-fetched aspect of the Herschel Walker mythology is true: He didn't work out with weights.

When he was 12, Walker asked local track and field coach Tom Jordan how he could get big and strong. Jordan answered, "Do push-ups, sit-ups and run sprints." Jordan didn't say how much to do, nor how often, just "regularly." To Walker, that meant a whole bunch every day. Within a year, he had done more than 100,000 push-ups and 100,000 sit-ups and had sprinted more than a million yards. After he added the grueling practices of his high school sports, he never stopped with his regimen, even tacking on some distance running.

By the time Walker was 17, he had "a physique that many body-builders would commit any number of unspeakable acts to possess." But he never took part in one of the most ubiquitous aspects of sports: weight training -- or none to speak of.

For one thing, Johnson County High in Wrightsville had no weights until Walker's senior year. "We finally scraped together enough money to get a few weights," a football coach recalled. The coaches were immediately curious to see how Walker would do. He grasped a 250-lb. barbell, pumped it a few times "like it was Styrofoam," put it down and said with genuine puzzlement,

BULLDOGS

"Coach, 250 ain't heavy." His coaches estimate that Walker spent no more than eight hours in the weight room that fall.

So how about Athens? He was strength tested with the rest of the players, but he never worked with the weights. The sensible consensus among the coaches was that the purpose of a weight program was to make an athlete strong, and "because Walker [was] already strong as a thousand-dollar mule, why tempt fate?"

It's true: Herschel Walker didn't work with weights.

The truth is often a slippery commodity in our daily lives. No, that dress doesn't make you look fat. But, officer, I wasn't speeding. I didn't get the project finished because I've been at the hospital every night with my ailing grandmother. What good-looking guy? I didn't notice.

Sometimes we lie to spare the feelings of others; more often, though, we lie to bail ourselves out of a jam, to make ourselves look better to others, or to gain the upper hand over someone.

But Jesus admonishes us to tell the truth. Frequently in our faith life we fret about what is right and what is wrong, but we can have no such ambivalence when it comes to telling the truth or lying.

God and his son are so closely associated with the truth that lying is ultimately attributed to the devil ("the evil one"). Given his character, God cannot lie; given his character, the devil lies as a way of life. Given your character, which is it?

Soon as I don't make gains, I'm going on a good weight program.
-- Herschel Walker when asked if he would ever train with weights

**Jesus declared himself to be the truth,
so whose side are we on when we lie?**

DAY 87

BLOOD TYPE

Read Hebrews 9:11-28.

"[W]ithout the shedding of blood there is no forgiveness"
(v. 22b).

The Dawgs truly did once have a coach who shed his blood for the Red and Black.

Writer Tim Hix declared Erk Russell was "the best hire [Vince Dooley] ever made." Bringing Russell on board as his defensive coordinator in January 1964 completed the assembling of Dooley's initial staff.

Russell was a stern disciplinarian who pushed his players to their limits, but he was also a loving father figure. "You'd run through a wall for that guy," said linebacker Frank Ros, captain of the 1980 national champions.

Russell was a genius at using gimmickry to inspire his troops. He had the idea of calling his defense "Junkyard Dawgs" to motivate them after a subpar season in 1974. He called Roger Dancz, the director of Georgia's Redcoat Marching Band, and asked him to play a few bars of Jim Croce's "Bad, Bad Leroy Brown" when the defense did something exceptional. In the spring before the 1980 national title season, he came up with the now-ubiquitous "Big Team, Little Me" T-shirt the team wore as a battle emblem.

But Russell's motivational masterpiece, that which made him forever a part of Bulldog lore, was accidental. In the late 1970s, during pregame warm-ups, he would butt his players' shoulder

BULLDOGS

pads with his bald head to get them fired up. End Robert Goodwin had just transferred from the offense and didn't know the drill. So he crashed into Russell's head with his helmet -- not once, but twice -- and blood began streaming down the coach's face.

The sight of that blood drove the players into a complete and total frenzy, and both a tradition and a legend were born.

Today, when we speak of sacrifice, we usually refer to the use of our time, talents, and possessions for the benefit of others. In the Bible, though, to our horror and dismay, we find an entire sacrificial system in which the surrendering of an animal's life is required. The blood acts as a purifying agent necessary for the forgiveness of sins, which dramatically and shockingly under-scores just how seriously God takes sin, even if we don't.

The death of Christ on the cross marked the beginning of the New Covenant, but not the end of the sacrificial system. Rather, it was the system's culmination. In other words, Christ's death -- whether on a cross or otherwise – wasn't novel at all; it was in keeping with the sacrificial system established on Mt. Sinai.

But it was vastly different. This was the Son of God who was slaughtered. He was the perfect sacrifice, rendering any other ineffectual and futile. God still requires the shedding of blood to forgive sins, but we don't have to slaughter pigeons, doves, and heifers. Instead, we have Jesus, who sacrificed himself for us.

I scabbed my head up in just two or three taps, and it would start bleeding again. It became a tradition.
-- Erk Russell on his bloody head-butting

Nothing but the blood of Jesus
makes forgiveness possible for us.

DAY 88

MYSTERIOUS WAYS

Read Romans 11:25-36.

*"O the depth of the riches and wisdom and knowledge
of God! How unsearchable are his judgments and how
inscrutable his ways!" (v. 33 NRSV)*

Dan Magill was such a fast typist that his speed was attributed
to God's moving in mysterious ways.

Magill, of course, is a Bulldog and University legend, widely
known throughout collegiate circles "for his unparalleled contributions to the Bulldog athletic program." Early on, Magill gained
a reputation as a prodigious typist. When he was in high school
and writing sports for the *Athens Banner-Herald*, one staff writer
Magill described as "a smart aleck" said of him, "That boy can't
write a lick but he sho' can type. God moves in mysterious ways."

In 1946, Magill worked for the *Atlanta Journal*, which held an
annual contest to determine the fastest typist for the national
newspaperman's competition. Magill was confident he would
win, but first he had to outduel the departmental competition and
perennial winner Ed Danforth, the veteran sports editor.

At high noon before a big crowd, the two faced off. They had
to type one sentence as many times as possible in two minutes.
Judging by the times the carriage bells rang, Magill was sure he
had won, but Danforth was declared the winner when the two
pages were compared. Magill was "flabbergasted, crestfallen."

Before the paper-wide competition the next day, Magill learned

BULLDOGS

that Danforth was sick and wanted him to represent the sports department. He was also made privy to a secret he was never to reveal: Danforth had cheated, typing a full page before the contest began. "You're the best we've ever had," Magill was told.

He set a personal record: 148 words a minute. With the good Lord moving in mysterious ways, that was enough to win both the local and the national competition.

"The good Lord sure moves in mysterious ways" is an old saying among people of faith, an acknowledgment of the limits of our understanding of God. This only serves to make God even more tantalizing because human nature loves a good mystery. We relish the challenge of uncovering what somebody else wants to hide whether it be on a TV show or in a rousing game of Clue.

Some mysteries are simply beyond our knowing, however. Events in our lives that are in actuality the mysterious ways of God remain so to us because we can't see the divine machinations. We can see only the results, appreciate that God was behind it all, and give him thanks and praise while renewing our trust in him.

God has revealed much about himself, especially through Jesus, but still much remains unknowable. Why does he tolerate the existence of evil? What does he really look like? Why is he so fond of bugs? What was the inspiration for chocolate?

We know for sure, though, that God is love, and so we proceed with life, assured that one day all mysteries will be revealed.

I only used two fingers: my left index finger and my right forefinger.
— Dan Magill on his 'mysterious' typing technique

**God keeps much about himself shrouded in
mystery, but one day we will see and understand.**

IMPOSSIBLE DREAMS

Read Matthew 19:16-26.

"Jesus looked at them and said, 'With man this is impossible, but with God all things are possible'" (v. 26).

Few times in UGA's long football history have dreams of a win seemed more impossible than they did on Oct. 6, 2001.

The Dawgs were in Knoxville to take on Tennessee. Consider, if you will, the circumstances that rendered a victory so impossible. Under veteran coach Phillip Fulmer, Tennessee was undefeated and ranked sixth nationally; under first-year head coach Mark Richt, the Dogs were 2-1 and unranked. Reggie Brown, Georgia's top receiver, was out for the season. Linebackers Will Witherspoon and Ryan Fleming were out with injuries; Boss Bailey was playing with a broken hand in a cast. Freshman quarterback David Greene would play his first road game in one of college footballs most boisterous and hostile atmospheres.

There was more. Georgia had not beaten Tennessee in Knoxville since Herschel Walker's freshman season: 1980. Many of the Georgia players hadn't even been born then. The Vols had not lost at home to an unranked team since 1992.

But there's more. Tennessee had the game's best rushing defense, giving up a mere 41 yards per game. The Vols had ten sacks to Georgia's three. The Dawg defense had made Arkansas' quarterback, a 30-percent passer, look like an All-America the week before. UT's quarterback was coming off a 309-yard game

BULLDOGS

against LSU.

Yet the Dawgs seemed to have done the impossible until UT pulled off an impossible play: a 62-yard screen pass for a touchdown and a 24-20 lead with only 44 seconds left. A Dawg win was certainly impossible now. Until with five seconds left, Greene hit fullback Verron Haynes in the end zone for an impossible touchdown on a play that will live in UGA football lore forever.

Impossibly, Georgia won 26-24.

Greene said that after the UT touchdown, Richt was confident Georgia could score. He knew his team wouldn't quit.

That's the way it is for Christians. We can't give up. Let's face it. Any pragmatic person, no matter how deep his faith, has to admit that we have succeeded in turning God's beautiful world into an impossible mess. The only hope for this dying, sin-infested place lies in our Lord's return to set everything right.

But we can't just give up and sit around praying for Jesus' return, as glorious a day as that will be. Our mission in this world is to change it for Jesus. We serve a Lord who calls us to step out in faith into seemingly impossible situations. We serve a Lord so audacious that he inspires us to believe that we are the instruments through which God does the impossible.

Changing the world may indeed seem impossible. Changing our corner of it, however, is not. It is, rather, a very possible, doable act of faith.

They are just too much for Georgia right now.
-- ESPN's Rece Davis, picking UT to win 34-14 in 2001

With God, nothing is impossible,
including changing the world for Jesus.

DAY 90

THE LONG HAUL

Read Luke 12:35-40.

"You also must be ready, because the Son of Man will come at an hour when you do not expect him" (v. 40).

They shared the same little-girl dream. Making that dream come true required that they never let go of it across the long haul that amounted to years.

Jasmine Hassell grew up in Lebanon, TN, Jasmine James in Memphis, and Anne Marie Armstrong in Norcross. From different backgrounds, they nevertheless shared a common dream: to play pro basketball. "Ever since I could remember, probably when I was about 6 or 7, I always wanted to play in the WNBA," James said. "Growing up, I think it's anyone's dream who plays basketball to be able to play in college," Armstrong said. "At the top of those dreams would be the opportunity to play professionally."

Making that dream come true meant years of preparation, untold hours of work, and excellence on the court and in the classroom for all three. They made it, winding up as Lady Bulldogs where the long haul continued with the relentless demands for excellence head coach Andy Landers places on his players.

The three excelled at UGA, becoming the 32nd, 33rd, and 34th 1,000-point career scorers in Lady Bulldogs' history. As a senior in 2012-13, Hassell was first-team All-SEC. James finished her career among the all-time leaders in five categories. Armstrong was first-team All-SEC as a junior who was hampered her senior

BULLDOGS

season by a high ankle sprain that wouldn't go away. They led the Lady Bulldogs to a 28-7 record in 2012-13 and within an overtime loss of the Final Four. With that defeat, the long haul was over.

But the dream was not. On Monday, April 15, 2013, the three were drafted by the WNBA. "It's just a blessing from God," Hassell declared. "I just thanked God" when she saw her name flash across her TV screen. "I felt really blessed," Armstrong said.

From childhood to the pros, Jasmine Hassell, Jasmine James, and Anne Marie Armstrong had made the long haul.

As those three Lady Dawgs showed, life is an endurance sport; you're in it for the long haul. So you schedule a physical, check your blood pressure for free at the pharmacy, walk or jog, and pull the treadmill out from under the bed and hop on.

The length of your life, however, is really the short haul when compared to the long haul that is eternity. To prepare yourself for eternity requires conditioning that is spiritual rather than physical. Jesus prescribed a regimen so his followers could be in tip-top spiritual shape. It requires not just occasional exercise but a way of living every day that includes abiding faith, decency, witnessing, mercy, trust, and generosity.

If the Dawgs aren't ready when the whistle first blows, they lose a game. If you aren't ready when Jesus calls, you lose eternity.

You think about it and dream about it when you're little and now 14-15 years later, you hear your name called.
-- Jasmine James on being drafted by the WNBA

Physical conditioning is good for the short run, but peak spiritual shape is necessary for the long haul.

DAY 91

OLD-FASHIONED

Read Leviticus 18:1-5.

"You must obey my laws and be careful to follow my decrees. I am the Lord your God" (v. 4).

Durward Pennington was such an old-fashioned football player that nobody today plays his position the way he did.

Pennington arrived in Athens in 1958 expecting to play quarterback. When he looked around, though, and saw Fran Tarkenton, Charlie Britt, and Tommy Lewis, he knew he wouldn't get many snaps under center. The team also had an experienced kicker, so Pennington figured he would spend most of his time as a Bulldog riding the bench and working on his degree.

But the kicker left school and turned pro. UGA backfield coach Sterling DuPree immediately drove down to Albany, looked his rising sophomore up, handed him a bag of balls, and told him to kick. Pennington did, so much so that over the summer his right leg grew two inches bigger than his left.

From 1959-61, Pennington was so reliable that he was nicknamed the "Automatic Toe." He led the Bulldogs in scoring all three seasons, and that automatic toe was the difference in three games the Dawgs won in 1961. He is, of course, most famous for the PAT he booted against Auburn in the legendary 14-13 win that clinched the 1959 SEC championship. (See Devotion No. 19.)

To watch a video today of Pennington, however, would be to take a true step back in time. That's because he was an "upright, square-toe-shoed, straight-on" kicker, a relic of the past compared to today's soccer-style kickers.

But he was good. Against Kentucky in 1961, he booted a 47-yard field goal. The Dawgs were offside, so he simply backed up five yards and slammed a 52-yarder through the uprights. Both kicks, of course, were nailed with his old-fashioned kicking style with its long, swinging leg action. Georgia won 16-15.

Usually, when we refer to some person, some idea, or some institution as old-fashioned, we deliver a full-fledged or at least thinly veiled insult. They're out of step with the times and the mores, hopelessly out of date, totally irrelevant, and quite useless.

For the people of God, however, "old-fashioned" is exactly the lifestyle we should pursue. The throwbacks are the ones who value honor, dignity, sacrifice, and steadfastness, who can be counted on to tell the truth and to do what they say. Old-fashioned folks shape their lives according to eternal values and truths, the ones handed down by almighty God.

These ancient laws and decrees are still relevant to contemporary life because they direct us to a lifestyle of holiness and righteousness that serves us well every single day. Such a way of living allows us to escape the ultimately hopeless life to which so many have doomed themselves in the name of being modern.

[Today's kickers] would view Pennington with such amusement that they think his type should be honored by a history museum.
-- Loran Smith on Durward Pennington's straight-on kicking style

The ancient lifestyle God calls us to still leads us
to a life of contentment, peace, and joy,
which never grows old-fashioned.

DAY 92

THE END

Read Revelation 22:1-17.

"I am the Alpha and the Omega, the First and the Last, the Beginning and the End" (v. 13).

Christian Robinson had one major problem with his career as a Bulldog football player: It had to end.

Robinson's time wearing the red and black ended with the 2013 Capital One Bowl. In the 45-31 Bulldog win, the senior linebacker had three solo tackles, including a quarterback sack. His time as a UGA student ended earlier, on Dec. 14, when Robinson joined six other Bulldog football players (present and past) -- Luis Capella, Sanders Commings, Terrence Edwards, Jonathan Owens, Bacarri Rambo, and Cornelius Washington -- in receiving their degrees.

Robinson "has definitely been a huge positive representation of what a college football player should be," said junior guard Dallas Lee, a close friend. "Christian has done a great job of just being a solid guy doing his job, being a good student and not getting in trouble. I don't think people celebrate that enough."

Robinson earned scholarships for his academics and was a regular volunteer for community service projects. On the field, he was never a star, but he was successful, playing in 51 of a possible 54 games, missing three with injuries.

It wasn't all good times for the all-state recruit out of Greater Atlanta Christian. After starting eleven games as a sophomore in 2010, a foot injury he suffered early in the 2011 season hampered him the rest of his career. He wound up moving from an every-game starter to a third-down middle linebacker in 2012. Plus, the home he shared with tight end Arthur Lynch, long snapper Ty Frix, quarterback Aaron Murray, and fullback Dustin Royston was vandalized after the loss to South Carolina in 2012.

Still, Robinson hated to see it all end. "If I could stay in this situation forever, I would," he said shortly before his graduation. "I love it here."

The privilege of playing football for the Georgia Bulldogs is just another example of one of life's basic truths: Everything ends. Even the stars have a life cycle, though admittedly it's extremely lengthy. Erosion eventually will wear a boulder to a pebble. Life itself is temporary; all living things have a beginning and an end.

Within the framework of our own lifetimes, we experience endings. Loved ones, friends, and pets die; relationships fracture; jobs dry up; our health, clothes, lawn mowers, TV sets – they all wear out. Even this world as we know it will end.

But one of the greatest ironies of God's gift of life is that not even death is immune from the great truth of creation that all things must end. That's because through Jesus' life, death, and resurrection, God himself acted to end any power death once had over life. In other words, because of Jesus, the end of life has ended. Eternity is ours for the claiming.

Coach Richt tells you that first day, 'you think it's going to last forever,' but it's over before you know it.

-- Christian Robinson

**Everything ends; thanks to Jesus Christ,
so does death.**

NOTES
(by Devotion Day Number)

1   It's amazing what our guys have done.": Patrick Garbin, *"Then Vince Said to Herschel . . ."* (Chicago: Triumph Books, 2007), p. 251.

1   It's amazing. That's . . . will never give up.: Garbin, p. 251.

2   a touchdown set up by . . . inside the Tech 10.: Vince Dooley with Loran Smith, *Dooley's Dawgs* (Atlanta: Longstreet Press, 2003), p. 69.

2   emptying its bench in the last five minutes,: Dooley with Smith, *Dooley's Dawgs*, p. 70.

2   At a ceremony the next . . . into the Chattahoochee River.: Dooley with Smith, *Dooley's Dawgs*, p. 70.

2   I was quite irritated.: Dooley with Smith, *Dooley's Dawgs*, p. 69.

3   "She was as impressive . . . it couldn't hurt us,": Vince Dooley with Blake Giles, *Tales from the 1980 Georgia Bulldogs* (Champaign, IL: Sports Publishing L.L.C., 2005), p. 35.

3   When Cavan mentioned . . . the plan up a year,": Dooley with Giles, *Tales from the 1980 Georgia Bulldogs*, p. 35.

3   "was a tremendous athlete in her own right.": Dooley with Giles, *Tales from the 1980 Georgia Bulldogs*, p. 35.

3   One of the things . . . let me beat Veronica.: Terry Todd, "'My Body's Like an Army,'" *Sports Illustrated*, Oct., 4, 1982, http://sportsillustrated.cnn.com/vault/article/magazine/MAG1125982/index.htm.

4   Vince Dooley really wanted . . . ice it down in the case.: Tony Barnhart, *Always a Bulldog* (Chicago: Triumph Books, 2011), p. 178.

4   the boys punched the . . . and their wives.: Barnhart, *Always a Bulldog*, p. 179.

4   the group politely insisted . . . let the door shut.: Barnhart, *Always a Bulldog*, p. 180.

4   We hadn't gotten away with anything.: Barnhart, *Always a Bulldog*, p. 180.

5   Brown knew he was . . . a little sprain maybe.: Chip Towers, "Georgia's Marlon Brown," *UGA sports blog*, Dec. 30, 2012, http://blogs.ajc.com/uga-sports-blog/2012/12/30/georgias-marlon-brown.

5   Never unlucky, never unfortunate. . . . I just roll with the punches.: Towers, "Georgia's Marlon Brown."

6   "Coach said some things . . . changed for us after that.": Roger Clarkson, "James' Putback Sends Lady Dogs to Sweet 16," *DOGbytesonline.com*, March 22, 2011, dogbytesonline.com/james-putback-sends-lady-dogs-to-sweet-16-43870.

6   During a time out, Landers . . . get on the boards.: Clarkson, "James' Putback Sends Lady Dogs to Sweet 16."

6   When the shot went . . . knock the shot in.: Clarkson, "James' Putback Sends."

7   "decent if subdued expectations." . . . his jersey number.: Rob Suggs, *Top Dawg* (Nashville: Thomas Nelson, 2008), p. 119.

7   "the kid was aggressive, . . . with surprising quickness.": Suggs, *Top Dawg*, p. 113.

7   "the coming-out party of [this] three-time All American.": Suggs, *Top Dawg*, p. 118.

7   "by some sleight of hand . . . moment it came out.: Suggs, *Top Dawg*, p. 118.

7   The bewildered USC quarterback . . . "Are you serious?": Suggs, *Top Dawg*, p. 118.

8   he threw his helmet into a trash can.: Seth Emerson, "Former Georgia Kicker Blair Walsh Experiencing Remarkable Turnaround," *Ledger-Enquirer*, Jan. 12, 2013, http://www.ledger-enquirer.com/2013/01/12/234126/former-georgia-kicker-blair-walsh.html.

8   Head coach Mark Richt eventually . . . kicker was "extremely hot.": Ben Wolk, "Blast from the Past: Senior Kicker Walsh," *The Red & Black*, Nov. 19, 2011, http://www.redandblack.com/sports/blast -from-the-past-senior-kicker-walsh.

8   "Your team giving you . . . like old times today.": Wolk, "Blast from the Past."

BULLDOGS

9   Over the years, he has . . . nicknamed him "The.": Tony Barnhart, *What It Means to Be a Bulldog* (Chicago: Triumph Books, 2004), p. 268.

9   Robinson was calmly going . . . answered. Kentucky called timeout.": Barnhart, *What It Means to Be a Bulldog*, p. 271.

9   In the 1981 Sugar Bowl, Robinson's . . . Dame's two return men.: Barnhart, *What It Means to Be a Bulldog*, p. 272.

9   Defensive coordinator Erk Russell called . . . onside kick in history.": Barnhart, *What It Means to Be a Bulldog*, p. 272.

9   When Scott got to midfield . . . being mobbed in the end zone.: Barnhart, *What It Means to Be a Bulldog*, p. 272.

9   My wife is from Michigan . . . She thinks it's really funny.: Barnhart, *What It Means to Be a Bulldog*, p. 273.

10 "I was on floor tumbling and . . . came the rebuilding of her confidence.: Roger Clarkson, "UGA's Earls on Road to Recovery," *OnlineAthens.com*, July 4, 2011. http://onlineathens.com/stories/070411/gym_85236044.shtml.

10 I wanted to be . . . part. I didn't know.: Clarkson, "UGA's Earls on Road to Recovery."

11 "probably the worst throw I've ever made in my life.": Marc Weiszer, "'Test of Toughness,'" *DOGbytesonline.com*, Oct. 31, 2012, http://dogbytesonline.com/test-of-toughness.

11 "You're going to have to win this ballgame,": Jonathan Branch, "Football Notebook: QB Murray Gets First Win," *DOGbytesonline.com*, Oct. 27, 2012, http://dogbytes online.com/football-notebook-qb-murray-gets-first-win.

11 A bad start is . . . at the quarterback position.: Weiszer, "'Test of Toughness.'"

12 The pregame publicity for the . . . the state's sports history.: Bill Cromartie, *Clean Old-Fashioned Hate* (Huntsville, AL: The Strode Publishers, Inc., 1977), p. 159.

12 The UGA band struck up "California, Here I Come": Cromartie, p. 160.

12 Georgia is the greatest team in the country.: Cromartie, p. 162.

13 "I thought [the umpire] was . . . pain from the plunking.: Roger Clarkson, "Dogs Prevail as Hogs Pitcher Plunks Cone," *DOGbytesonline,com*. May 2, 2011, dogbyptesonline.com/dogs-prevail-as-hogs-pitcher-plunks-cone/45248/.

13 Zach shook his hand . . . it looked like it did.: Clarkson, "Dogs Prevail."

14 I didn't think it would . . . or something like that.: Ken Bradley, "Georgia's Todd Gurley Drawing Early Comparisons to Herschel Walker," *Sporting News*, Oct. 3, 2012, aol.sportingnews.com/ncaa-football/story/2012-10-03/todd-gurley-georgia.

15 "frantically motioning and screaming for his players to stay down.": Garbin, pp. 211-12.

15 Linebacker Mitch Davis admitted . . . and run another play. Garbin, p. 212.

16 In a gloomy, deserted . . . of other people's enjoyment.": Suggs, *Top Dawg*, p. 19.

16 when his head coach asked . . . I sure believe in football.": Suggs, *Top Dawg*, p. 28.

16 This morning, though, he . . . get back into football.: Suggs, *Top Dawg*, pp. 19-20.

17 He said he turned off . . . "Did he say old man?": Marc Weiszer, "Missouri DT Gets in First Verbal Jabs," *DOGbytesonline.com*, Sept. 2, 2012, http://dogbytesonline.com/mizzou-dt- gets-in-first-verbal-jabs.

17 Even Richt's mother reacted . . . he thought about it.: Marc Weiszer, "Quick Hits: Dawson Yet to Meet with NCAA," *DOGbytesonline.com*, Sept. 5, 2012, http://dog bytesonline.com/quick-hits-dawson-yet-to-meet.

17 UGA quarterback Aaron Murray . . . a little added incentive.": Marc Weiszer, "Welcome to the SEC," *DOGbytesonline.com*, Sept. 9, 2012. http://dogbytesonline.com/welcome-to-the-sec.

17 In their raucous locker . . . "Grown Man Football.": Marc Weiszer, "Dogs Showed 'Mental, Physical Toughness,'": *DOGbytesonline.com*, Sept. 9, 2012, http://dogbytesonline.com/dogs-showed-mental-physical-toughness-in-win.

MORE GEORGIA

17   I don't know what he meant . . . and do what we do well.: Weiszer, "Mizzou DT Gets in First Verbal Jabs."

18   "a good football player.": Vince Dooley with Blake Giles, *Vince Dooley's Tales from the 1980 Georgia Bulldogs* (Champaign, IL: Sports Publishing L.L.C., 2005), p. 80.

18   At practice Monday, McMickens' . . . "ruining the morale of the team.": Dooley with Giles, *Vince Dooley's Tales*, p. 80.

18   Dooley summoned the disappointed player . . . We need you. We really do.": Dooley with Giles, *Vince Dooley's Tales*, p. 81.

18   "He became our best special teams player,": Dooley with Giles, *Vince Dooley's Tales*, p. 80.

18   I don't believe we would have won the national championship without him.: Dooley with Giles, *Vince Dooley's Tales*, p. 81.

19   they were "bad at everything but winning.": "Bad at Everything But Winning," *Sports Illustrated*, Sept. 19, 1966, http://vault.sportsillustrated.cnn.com/vault/article/magazine/MAG1079032/index.htm.

19   The '59 squad was pretty . . . to the next game.": "Bad at Everything But Winning."

19   it was their quality . . . yards the team needed.: "Bad at Everything But Winning."

19   Up front were fellows . . . anything but winning.: "Bad at Everything But Winning."

20   "I thought early emotion got the better part of us,": Marc Weiszer, "Bulldogs Reach 20 Wins," *OnlineAthens.com*, March 3, 2011, http://www.onlineathens.com/stories/030311/mens/793735967.shtml.

20   I'd argue all day . . . for the last time.: Weiszer, "Bulldogs Reach 20 Wins."

20   It's a big deal for . . . 20 mark is pretty special.: Weiszer, "Bulldogs Reach 20 Wins."

21   In 2009, *Sporting News* tabbed Curran, a junior linebacker, the SEC's best hitter: "Rennie Curran," *georgiadogs.com*, http://www.nmnathletics.com/ViewArticledbm/?DB_OEM_ID=88008&ATCLI1.

21   "the most dominant defensive player in the game.": "Rennie Curran," *Wikipedia, the free encyclopedia*, en.wikipedia.org/wiki/Rennie_Curran.

21   Curran's family came to . . . years -- Curran went home.: "Curran Returns to Native Land," *DOGbytesonline.com*, Athens-Banner-Herald, April 26, 2011.

21   That was my dream . . . had never met before.: "Curran Returns to Native Land,"

22   when the Gator head coach . . . I was registered in school,": Barnhart, *What It Means to Be a Georgia Bulldog*, p. 16.

22   Seeking a teacher's certificate, . . . St. John flunked it: Barnhart, *What It Means to be a Georgia Bulldog*, pp. 17-18.

22   I understand some of the Florida coaches caught [flak].: Barnhart, *What I Means to Be a Bulldog*, p. 18.

23   A disconsolate Lumpkin stood on the sideline, his head down.: Paul Newberry, "Capital One Bowl 2004," www.mmbolding.com/bowls/Capital_One_2004.html.

23   "Forget about it," . . . help us win this thing.": Suggs, *Top Dawg*, p. 159.

23   Not in my huddle.: Suggs, *Top Dawg*, p. 159.

24   "a pair without peer, . . . backcourt in NCAA history.": Franz Lidz, "Mirror, Mirror," *Sports Illustrated*, Nov. 15, 1999, http://sportsillustrated.cnn.com/vault/article/magazine/MAG1017687/index.htm.

24   They wore similar clothes, . . . communication at all.: Lidz, "Mirror, Mirror."

24   At times Kelly and Coco . . . of a single personality.: Lidz, "Mirror, Mirror."

25   He was "just another . . . Southern California gym." Jordan Conn, "Dogged Pursuit," *ESPN The Magazine*, Oct. 4, 2012, http://espn.go.com/college-football/story/_/id/8448679/georgia-bulldogs-lb-jarvis-jones.

25   The first doctor told . . . "Coach, I'm a Dawg,": Conn, "Dogged Pursuit."

25   I understand you never . . . to be taken away.: Conn, "Dogged Pursuit."

26   On the play, end Dicky . . . knew they were beat.": Barnhart, *What I Means to Be a Bulldog*, p. 192.

26   didn't know much about . . . got the Dogs interested.: Barnhart, *What I Means to Be a Bulldog*, p. 188.

26   Maryland pushed all the . . . made up his mind.: Barnhart, *What I Means to Be a Bulldog*, p. 189.

26   I was leaning toward Georgia, but that [phone call] sealed the deal.: Barnhart, *What It Means to Be a Bulldog*, p. 189.

27   he eagerly accepted the . . . roof over his head.: Loran Smith, "Zippy Morocco Celebrates 60 Years," *GeorgiaDogs.com*, Feb. 28, 2013, www.georgiadogs.com/sports/m-baskbl/spec-rel/022813aaa.html.

27   Trailing by one, Georgia . . . out of the basket": Dan Magill, "Bulldogs' Zippy Morocco Shocked Vols," *OnlineAthens.com*, Feb. 23, 1999, onlineathens.com/stories/022399/dog_022399032.shtml.

27   The next day, Tennessee's . . . on here last night,": Smith, "Zippy Morocco Celebrates."

27   Although we hated losing . . . your outstanding performance.: Smith, "Zippy Morocco Celebrates."

28   When Dooley made the offer . . . a position at Tennessee.: Dooley with Giles, *Tales from the 1980 Georgia Bulldogs*, p. 12.

28   This concerned the boss . . . with the Georgia program.: Dooley with Giles, *Tales from the 1980 Georgia Bulldogs*, pp. 12, 14.

28   When the Bulldog staff . . . coached me up on it.": Dooley with Giles, *Tales from the 1980 Georgia Bulldogs*, p. 14.

28   Bill Lewis knew what all 22 guys were doing on every play.: Dooley with Giles, *Tales from the 1980 Georgia Bulldogs*, p. 15.

29   something was wrong . . . He was saved that night.: Chris Arnzen, ""Alec Millen," *Iron Sharpens Iron*, Nov. 19, 2008, sharpens.blogsports.com/2008/11/mp3-available-here_19.html.

29   God, if I can know you . . . I will do anything.: Arnzen, "Alec Millen."

30   "The first dominant player of the Vince Dooley era,": Rob Doster and Kevin Daniels, eds., *Game Day Georgia Football* (Chicago: Triumph Books, 2005), p. 47.

30   "a slow quarterback with . . . with no foot speed.": Barnhart, *Always a Bulldog*, p. 304.

30   In the fall of 1962, . . . let him anticipate plays,: Barnhart, *Always a Bulldog*, p. 305.

30   After the last UGA defensive . . . and not to ridicule them.: Barnhart, *Always a Bulldog*, p. 309.

30   I thought he was kidding.: Barnhart, *Always a Bulldog*, p. 309.

31   "It got a little scary at points,": Marc Weiszer, "Wild Escape," *DOGbytesonline.com*, Oct. 20, 2012, http://dogbytesonline.com/wild-escape.

31   "The extra points shouldn't be that way,": "Football Notebook: Special Teams Flirt with Disaster," *DOGbytesonline.com*, Oct. 20, 2012, http://dogbytesonline.com/football-notebook-special-teams.

31   "I think (Morgan) has . . . if he was sure.": "Football Notebook: Special Teams Flirt."

31   I think against Florida we'll play a lot better.: Weiszer, "Wild Escape."

32   When they began tearing . . . innocent Georgia bystanders.": Garbin, p. 198.

32   It was the first time . . . cannons for crowd control.: Garbin, p. 199.

33   a jersey that lacked . . . had earned a scholarship.: Chris Starrs, "UGA Snapper Frix Has a Story to Tell," *DOGbytesonline.com*, Dec. 29, 2012, http://dogbytesonline.com/uga-snapper-frix-has-a-story-to-tell.

33   That was something you never even dream about.: Starrs, "UGA Snapper Frix Has a Story to Tell."

34   "I'll tell you what; . . . near the 17th hole.: Chris White, "UGA Coaches Go Out of Their Way," *DOGbytesonline.com*, May 6, 2012, http://dogbytesonline.com/uga-coaches-go-out.

34   "We were behind a . . . champion to congratulate him.: White, "UGA Coaches Go Out Of Their Way."

34 He knows us well enough to know we're very superstitious.: "UGA Coaches Go Out Of Their Way."

35 "I don't think I threw . . . threw the ball terrible.": Ron Higgins, "SEC Traditions: Bobo Knows How to 'Bowl' Them Over," *SEC Digital Network*, Dec. 29, 2010, http://www.secdigitalnetwork.com/SECNation/SECTraditions/tabid/1073.

35 "My last college pass . . . a good day.": Higgins, "SEC Traditions: Bobo Knows How."

35 It was one of those days when I couldn't miss.: Higgins, "SEC Traditions: Bobo Knows How."

36 Robinson made recruiting visits . . . was a big Dawg fan.: Barnhart, *What I Means to Be a Bulldog*, p. 212.

36 "around a university and a town I really love.": Barnhart, *What It Means to Be a Bulldog*, p. 215.

36 I knew I could get a good education at Georgia.: Barnhart, *What It Means to Be a Bulldog*, p. 214.

37 the play was a . . . designed to exploit that.: Vince Dooley, *Dooley's Play Book* (Athens: Hill Street Press, 2008), pp. 136-37.

37 the Tide line up just . . . catch in the corner.: Dooley, *Dooley's Play Book*, p. 136.

37 He had lost track . . . must be in trouble, too.": Dooley, *Dooley's Play Book*, p. 137.

37 We got to kick the extra point!: Dooley, *Dooley's Play Book*, p. 137.

38 "You can't get any lower . . . "We expected to win.": Tim Tucker, "Who's Top Dog All-Time in Games Played?" *UGA sports blog*, Dec. 24, 2012, http://blogs.ajc.com/uga-sports-blog/2012/12/24/whos-top-dog-all-time-in-games-played.

38 "I think my class . . . gotten that [swagger] back.": Tucker, "Who's Top Dog All-Time?"

38 We're leaving behind . . . in the right direction.: Tucker, "Who's Top Dog All-Time?"

39 [Vince Dooley] once said that . . . appeared in one game.: Dooley with Giles, *Tales from the 1980 Georgia Bulldogs*, p. 103.

39 never missing a day of . . . the farm with his father.: Dooley with Giles, *Tales from the 1980 Georgia Bulldogs*, p. 103.

39 At practice, All-SEC defensive . . . just innocently doing that,": Dooley with Giles, *Tales from the 1980 Georgia Bulldogs*, p. 104.

39 After he left Athens, . . . him out of his lungs.: Dooley with Giles, *Tales from the 1980 Georgia Bulldogs*, p. 105.

39 "If there was ever going to be a hero, he is my hero.": Dooley with Giles, *Tales from the 1980 Georgia Bulldogs*, p. 105.

39 Here I am fixing to kick the bucket and I'm watching *The Flintstones*.: Dooley with Giles, *Tales from the 1980 Georgia Bulldogs*, p. 105.

40 "We were getting crushed," . . . and started from scratch.": Marc Weiszer, "Fox Has Strong Ties," *OnlineAthens.com*, March 16, 2011, http://onlineathens.com/stories/031611/men_800334874.shtml.

40 Mark launched a friendship . . . Huskies' promotion department.: "Mark Fox Profile," www.georgiadogs.com/sports/m-baskbl/mtt/fox_mark00.html.

40 The two started dating. . . . cost a lot of money.": Weiszer, "Fox Has Strong Ties."

40 It was a great time, . . . what they were doing.: Weiszer, "Fox Has Strong Ties."

41 Injuries and academic casualties . . . and how to get open.: Barnhart, *What It Means to Be a Bulldog*, p. 164.

41 "All I did was block,": Barnhart, *What It Means to Be a Bulldog*, p. 165.

41 The Gators were packing . . . called it a fire drill.": Barnhart, *What It Means to Be a Bulldog*, p. 166.

41 It was really great . . . out of that place.: Barnhart, *What It Means to Be a Bulldog*, p. 166.

42 Orphaned at 14 and . . . to his former coach.: Andrew Conrad, "Years Later, Colt Fans Still Seek out Art DeCarlo," *explorehoward.com*, May 4, 2011, http://archives.explorehoward.com/news/83979/years-later.

42 what Butts saw was . . . offer him a scholarship.: Gene Asher, "Meet 'Mr. Nice Guy,'"

Georgia Trend, Nov. 2004, www.georgiatrend.com/November-2004/meet-mr-nice-guy.

42   Bodine "gave my dad" . . . and said 'good luck.'": Conrad, "Years Later."
42   had the Bulldog football team . . . won by a landslide.": Asher, "Meet 'Mr. Nice Guy.'"
42   Art DeCarlo was one . . . for the Red and Black.: Asher, "Meet 'Mr. Nice Guy.'"
43   "the SEC Coach of the . . . late to make amends.: Suggs, *Top Dawg*, p. 150.
43   That didn't matter; this had to be made right.: Suggs, *Top Dawg*, pp. 150-51.
43   The weary head coach . . . an extended autograph session.: Suggs, *Top Dawg*, p. 151.
43   The 'no-huddle' lifestyle had caught up with him.: Suggs, *Top Dawg*, p. 150.
44   Outlined against a backdrop . . . horseman rode again.": Loran Smith, "Jones' Perfor-
       mance Against Florida Best All-Time in Series," *DOGbytesonline.com*, Oct. 30,
       2012, http://dogbytesonline.com/loran-smith-jarvis-jones-performance.
44   a game that matched . . . and Bill Stanfill.: Smith, "Jones' Performance."
44   With the emergence of . . . where the ball was,": Smith, "Jones' Performance."
44   "played like he was lined up in the Gator backfield.": Smith, "Jones' Performance."
44   [In] Bulldog history, there . . . on at EverBank Field.: Smith, "Jones' Performance."
45   "Georgia was in a desperate situation.": Dooley with Smith, *Dooley's Dawgs*, p. 7.
45   university president O.C. Aderhold . . . announcing his hiring.: Dooley with Smith,
       Dooley's Dawgs, p. 2.
45   The athletic board was described . . . downcast at the hiring: Dooley with Smith,
       Dooley's Dawgs, p. 1.
45   On the first play, future All-American . . . week, 'What did you expect?'": Dooley with
       Smith, *Dooley's Dawgs*, p. 8.
45   I was left alone in . . . want to know me.: Dooley with Smith, *Dooley's Dawgs*, p. 41.
46   "I was terrified," . . . He was in.": Roger Clarkson, "Cornerback Cuff Doesn't Boast,"
       OnlineAthens.com, Aug. 9. 2010, http://www.onlineathens.com/stories/080910/
       foo_692591872.shtml.
46   "It looked like he . . . out of a cannon,": Clarkson, "Cornerback Cuff Doesn't Boast."
46   He recalled his own experience . . . try to keep guys up,": Clarkson, "Cornerback Cuff
       Doesn't Boast."
46   "ambivalent, vacillating, impulsive, unsubmissive.": John MacArthur, *Twelve Ordi-
       nary Men* ((Nashville: W Publishing Group, 2002), p. 39.
46   "the greatest preacher . . . birth of the church.: MacArthur, *Twelve Ordinary Men*, p. 39.
46   It's about keeping . . . and setting an example.: Clarkson, "Cornerback Cuff Doesn't
       Boast."
47   His mother frequently reminded . . . I was actually good at,": Roger Clarkson, "Big
       Man, Big Plans," *DOGbytesonline.com*, Oct. 19, 2012, http://dogbytes.com/big-
       man-big-plans.
47   "That's for real," . . . I was at football,": Clarkson, "Big Man, Big Plans."
47   I don't know what bike . . . that could hold him.: Clarkson, "Big Man, Big Plans."
48   "I just never enjoyed it . . . 100 percent at peace,": Ron Higgins, "SEC Traditions: It
       Was Always Easy Being Greene," *SEC Digital Network*, Sept. 27, 2012, http://
       www.secdigitalnetwork.com/SECNation/SECTraditions/tabid/1073/Article.
48   I just loved the feel of college and high school ball.: Higgins, "SEC Traditions: It was
       Always Easy."
49   "I didn't look at any . . . wants to be part of.": Scott Bernarde, "UGA Equestrian Team
       Set to Defend National Title," *ajc.com*, March 25, 2010, http://www.ajc.com/
       sports/uga/uga-equestrian-team.
49   She wore a coral-. . . . to be successful.: Bernarde, "UGA Equestrian Team."
49   I was all red and black.: Bernarde, "UGA Equestrian Team."
50   When head coach Wally Butts . . . 162 pounds in high school.: Barnhart,
       Always a Bulldog, p. 239.
50   he put on two bulky . . . as long as you wish.": Barnhart, *Always a*

Bulldog, p. 240.

50 I started eating the good food they served us at the dorm and started gaining some weight.: Barnhart, *Always a Bulldog,* p. 240.

51 The coaches couldn't decide . . . That was the call.: Barnhart, *What It Means to Be a Bulldog,* pp. 234-35.

51 Wisdom glanced around . . . run that out route.": Barnhart, *What It Means to Be a Bulldog,* p. 235.

51 I managed to contribute a little bit to our win.: Barnhart, *What It Means to Be a Bulldog,* p. 234.

52 "He was the best option we had,": Roger Clarkson, "Dogs' Gentle Giant," *DOGbytes online.com,* Aug. 9, 2011, http://dogbytesonline.com/dogs-gentle-giant-47490.

52 receiver Tavarres King admitted, "kind . . . to kill me every day.": Clarkson, "Dogs' Gentle Giant."

52 "He's a great guy . . . and stuff like that,": Clarkson, "Dogs' Gentle Giant."

52 I'm not the type of . . . to smile all the time.: Clarkson, "Dogs' Gentle Giant."

53 Among those cheering on . . . for Women in Tallahassee,: Loran Smith, "1931 Georgia-Florida Game One for the Books," *DOGbytesonline.com,* Oct. 29, 2010, http://dogbytesonlin.com/smith/1931-georgia-florida-game.

53 In his first-ever . . . it's Buster Mott.": Jesse Outlar, *Between the Hedges* (Huntsville, AL: The Strode Publishers, 1974), p. 45.

54 "We needed to get some . . . after losing two straight,": Roger Clarkson, "Lady Dogs Prevail in OT," *DOGbytesonline.com,* Feb. 4, 2011, http://dogbytesonline.com/lady-dogs-prevail-in-ot-42000.

54 We were able to stay the course and get the win.: Clarkson, "Lady Dogs Prevail."

55 Picked by one forecaster to battle Vanderbilt for the SEC cellar,": Garbin, p. 158.

55 Uga III stood at midfield . . . we got 'em tonight.'": Ron Higgins, "SEC Traditions: Uga VIII," *SEC Digital Network,* Oct. 22, 2010, http://www.secdigitalnetwork.com/SECNation/SECTraditions/tabid/1073/Article/21644.

55 I was so excited . . . our team what I saw.: Higgins, "UGA VIII."

56 Milton was only 9 when . . . chance to be somebody.: Garbin, p. 233.

56 "the loudest I've probably . . . during one single play.": Robert Bruce, "College Running Back Turned Pro Golfer?" *Game Under Repair,* Feb. 16, 2009. gameunder repair.wordpresss.com/2009/2002/16/college-running-back-turned-pro-golfer/.

56 Hey, coming from where . . . car had leather seats.: Garbin, p. 233.

57 some of the players "maintained . . . a tremendous opportunity.": Dooley with Giles, *Tales from the 1980 Georgia Bulldogs,* pp. 126-27.

57 "I remember feeling total . . . to lose to those guys.": Dooley with Giles, *Tales from the 1980 Georgia Bulldogs,* p. 127.

57 "I didn't think that we were . . . It ain't over yet,": Dooley with Giles, *Tales from the 1980 Georgia Bulldogs,* p. 128.

57 "I could just see the . . . looking real doubtful.": Dooley with Giles, *Tales from the 1980 Georgia Bulldogs,* p. 127.

57 Center Joe Happe said it felt like "third and a million.": Dooley with Giles, *Tales from the 1980 Georgia Bulldogs,* p. 128.

57 I felt like we had blown our undefeated hopes.: Dooley with Giles, *Tales from the 1980 Georgia Bulldogs,* p. 127.

58 "I was devastated," she said. . . . considering dropping gymnastics.: Suzanne Yoculan & Bill Donaldson, *Perfect 10* (Athens: Hill Street Press, 2006), pp. 40-41.

58 Fed up by the rejection, . . . the future Hall-of-Famer's mind.: Yoculan & Donaldson, pp. 41-42.

58 "I just don't think . . . gym with the men's team.: Yoculan & Donaldson, pp. 42-43.

58 McMinn, "who knew more . . . not to axe the sport.: Yoculan & Donaldson, p. 41.

58   "despicable, vile, unprincipled scoundrels.": MacArthur, p. 152.

58   I'm not interested. I did not even apply.: Yoculan & Donaldson, p. 41.

59   Dan Magill was seated . . . and agility than Lawrence.": Dan Magill, "Lawrence Deserving of Cotton Bowl Hall of Fame," *OnlineAthens.com*, Jan. 27, 2003, http://onlineathens.com/stories/012703/dog_20030127027.shtml.

59   I see what you mean!: Magill, "Lawrence Deserving of Cotton Bowl Hall of Fame."

60   He received his first real . . . pro day in March 2011.: Marc Weiszer, "Durham 'Speechless' in Seattle," *OnlineAthenscom*, May 1, 2011, http://onlineathens.com/stories/050111/foo_822578051.shtml.

60   he just wanted to hear his named called.: Loran Smith, "Durham's Life After a Bulldog Football Player," georgiadogs.com, Jan. 19, 2011, http://www.georgiadogs.com/sports/m-footbl/spec-rel/011911aaa.html.

60   I was speechless when it happened.: Weiszer, "Durham 'Speechless' in Seattle."

61   Oh, Lord," Khaalidah Miller . . . teams in the country.: "Miller Scores Career-High 25," *DOGbytesonline.com*, Feb. 3, 2013, http://dogsbytesonline.com/miller-scores.

61   As the 2012-13 season . . . case of an emergency.: "Miller Scores Career-High 25."

61   "I always kind of . . . the one to control the floor,": "Miller Scores Career-High 25."

61   I've just been working . . . and play the position.: "Miller Scores Career-High 25."

62   Dooley figured the percentage . . . to dictate his preference." Loran Smith, "Athens' Amp Arnold Was Hometown Hero," *DOGbytesonline.com*, Nov. 23, 2012. http://dogbytesonline.com/loran-smith-athens-amp-arnold.

62   I saw Buck was in trouble, I turned upfield.: Smith, "Athens' Amp Arnold Was Hometown Hero."

63   that little bit of history slipped by the elder Dooley,: Ron Higgins, "SEC Traditions: The Dooley Family Tree," *SEC Digital Network*, Sept. 2, 2010, http://www.secdigitalnetwork.com/SECNation/SECTraditions/tabid/1073/Article/134279.

63   he never really expected . . . be a football coach.: Higgins, "The Dooley Family Tree."

63   had loved the game even as "a pipsqueak,": Higgins, "The Dooley Family Tree."

63   The head Bulldog had a . . . having a little fun!": Higgins, "The Dooley Family Tree."

64   Mark Richt was reluctant . . . the kick. Richt relented.: Garbin, p. 243.

64   I was holding that . . . away from me.: Garbin, p. 244.

65   Kent Lawrence rushed onto . . . on a sheet of paper.: Garbin, p. 123.

65   He had not even practiced at the position.: Garbin, p. 124.

65   "You'd never know he'd. . . the control in spectacular fashion.": *Garbin*, p. 124.

66   "He couldn't run fast," . . . ever broke five-flat,": Dooley with Giles, p. 75.

66   the first coach he . . . making the linemen look bad.: Dooley with Giles, p. 75.

66   "I couldn't find anybody else . . . I ran him in .": Dooley with Giles, p. 76.

66   How does this guy . . . so you play him.: Dooley with Giles, p. 74.

67   When the UGA offensive . . . shorter than everybody else.: Beau Cabell, "UGA's Andrews Isn't the Tallest Center," *Macon Telegraph*, Aug. 4, 2012, http://www.macon.com/2012/08/04/2123100/ugas-andrews-isnt-the-tallest.html.

67   he is taller and heavier than bout 90 percent of the general U.S. population.: Cabell, "UGA's Andrews Isn't the Tallest Center."

67   Offensive line coach . . . you to work harder.": Cabell, "UGA's Andrews Isn't the Tallest Center."

67   In high school at . . . fight in the dog.": Cabell, "UGA's Andrews Isn't the Tallest Center."

67   There's nothing I can . . . God blessed me with.: Cabell, "UGA's Andrews Isn't the Tallest Center."

68   "regarded as perhaps the best team ever at Florida.": Garbin, p. 149.

68   With everyone on his . . . had not warmed up.: Garbin, p. 151.

69   Lizzy Stemke hadn't gotten over . . . call came for another.: Roger Clarkson, "Whirlwind of Change Accompanies Stemke," *Online*

Athens.com, Jan. 27, 2011, onlineathens.com/stories/012711/vol_776679438.shtml.

69 She really hadn't planned for two . . . the trip to scout Athens out.: Clarkson, "Whirlwind of Change."

69 Let's do it all at once.: Clarkson, "Whirlwind of Change."

70 "If you blinked, you would have missed it,": Ron Higgins, "SEC Traditions: Pollack Is Still a Showstopper," *SEC Digital Network,* Dec. 9, 2011, http://www.sec digitalnetwork.com/SECNationSECTraditions/tabid/1073/Article/229991.

70 "He never played another snap . . . he was 6 years old.: Higgins, "Pollack Is Still."

70 "he was emotionally well-equipped . . . fingers and other health issues.: Higgins, "Pollack Is Still."

70 "I feel incredibly blessed to have what I have,": Higgins, "Pollack Is Still."

70 God never closes one door without opening another one.: Higgins, "Pollack Is Still."

71 "In 1962, the Bulldogs' running . . . worst in Georgia history.": Garbin, p. 110.

71 In the locker room . . . sure you can intercept.": Garbin, p. 110.

71 the second-longest in school history at the time: Garbin, p. 110.

71 If you miss that ball, it'll be an Auburn touchdown.: Garbin, p. 110.

72 In the summer of 1939, . . . recruiting trip to Athens.: Mark Lancaster, "No. 3: University of Georgia Athlete of the Century: Frank Sinkwich," Ken Samelson, ed., *Echoes of Georgia Football* (Chicago: Triumph Books, 2006), pp. 47-48.

72 Before he agreed to play . . . The coaches didn't hesitate.: Lancaster, p. 48.

73 a Sunday school message . . . resonated with them.: Brian Curtis, "Faith in the Game," *Echoes of Georgia Football,* Ken Samelson, ed. (Chicago: Triumph Books, 2006), p. 135.

73 "While our sons, . . . we doing to help?": J. Gerald Harris, "Katharyn Richt: Preseason and Postseason #1-Ranked Mom," *The Christian Index,* May 7, 2009, http://www.christianindex.org/5431.article.

73 About the same time, . . . a facial deformity.: Curtis, "Faith in the Game," p. 135.

73 Mark recalled asking himself . . . maybe we should,": Harris, "Katharyn Richt."

73 "Anya was so small and . . . what age or how long.": Harris, "Katharyn Richt."

73 "I am thankful that . . . gained more than they have.": Harris, "Katharyn Richt."

73 You can't just talk about . . . was our part.: Curtis, "Faith in the Game," p. 136.

74 "I was under the radar recruiting-wise,": Tim Tucker, "Former Walk-On McPhee Living His Dream as a Bulldog," *The Atlanta Journal-Constitution,* March 10,2010, http://www.ajc.com/sports/uga/former-walk-on-mcphee-361152.html.

74 "He's a guy who . . . try to earn some respect.": Tucker, "Former Walk-On McPhee."

74 "We call him 'McThree,'" . . . a major minutes guy.": Tucker, "Former Walk-On McPhee."

74 I think he's the . . . on our team by far.: Tucker, "Former Walk-On McPhee."

75 "He just threw a . . . kind of a busted play.": Marc Weiszer, "Capital W," *DOGbytes online.com,* Jan. 1, 2013, http://www.dogbytesonline.com/capital-w.

75 He sings and plays . . . and likes to draw.: Loran Smith, "Bulldogs' WR Conley a Man of Many Talents," *DOGbytesonline.com,* Feb. 23, 2011, http://dogbytesonline.com/smith-bulldogs-wr-conley.

75 Mike Bobo guessed Nebraska . . . delivered the ball,": Loran Smith, "Georgia Caps Season," *DOGbytesonline.com,* Jan. 7, 2013, http://dogbytesonline.com/loran-smith-georgia-caps-season.

75 It was either going to be a huge play or a bust.: Weiszer, "Capital W."

76 "Auburn helped us," . . . care how it comes.": Roger Clarkson, "Four-Run Sixth Inning Lifts Georgia over Auburn in Opener," *DOGbytesonline.com,* May 4, 2012, http://dogbytesonline.com/four-run-sixth-inning.

76 We didn't get any hits, but guys had really good at-bats.: Clarkson, "Four-Run Sixth Inning Lifts Georgia."

77 he struggled that first quarter . . . academic load and football.: Barnhart, *What It*

Means to Be a Bulldog, p. 105.

77   "I kept plugging along,": Barnhart, *What It Means to Be a Bulldog*, p. 106.

77   Shortly before the '65 . . . was scared to death,": Barnhart, *What It Means to Be a Bulldog*, p. 106.

77   Chewing on his omnipresent . . . starting for me than you.": Barnhart, *What It Means to Be a Bulldog*, pp. 106-07.

77   The coach was lying, . . . up to play,": Barnhart, *What It Means to Be a Bulldog*, p. 107.

77   If my grandmother had . . . Granny, here it comes.': Barnhart, *What It Means to Be a Bulldog*, p. 107.

78   "They haven't played a good . . . became "verbal kudzu";: Suggs, *Top Dawg*, p. 120.

78   played "smash-mouth, . . . country boys played,": Suggs, *Top Dawg*, p. 121.

78   If they come over and . . . they go back to Athens.: Suggs, *Top Dawg*, p. 120.

79   The day before the 1978 . . . in a perfect Dooley.: Dooley with Giles, *Tales from the 1980 Georgia Bulldogs*, p. 156.

79   The players fell out, . . . better do it tomorrow.": Dooley with Giles, *Tales from the 1980 Georgia Bulldogs*, p. 157.

79   Everybody couldn't stop laughing and talking.: Dooley with Giles, *Tales from the 1980 Georgia Bulldogs*, p. 157.

80   an invitation he has always . . . he could think of at the moment.: Loran Smith, *Wally's Boys* (Athens: Longstreet Press, 2005), p. 48.

80   he entered the all-star . . . him a football scholarship.: Smith, *Wally's Boys*, p. 49.

80   "most dramatic touchdown play" in Georgia football history.": Loran Smith, cited by Vince Dooley in *Dooley's Playbook*, p. 7.

80   I thought about those . . . and kept my mouth shut.: Smith, *Wally's Boys*, p. 48.

81   her head coach described . . . Georgia women's tennis team": Marc Weiszer, "Kowase Keeps Georgia Women Alive," *DOGbytesonline.com*, May 12, 2012, http://dogbytesonline.com/kowase-keeps-georgia-women-alive.

81   "She wasn't playing bad," . . . absolutely outplaying her.": Weiszer, "Kowase Keeps Georgia Women Alive."

81   When Kowase got within . . . would win the match.: Weiszer, "Kowase Keeps Georgia Women Alive."

81   "Just simply amazing . . . Call mama, of course.: Weiszer, "Kowase Keeps Georgia Women Alive."

81   She is such a fighter.: Weiszer, "Kowase Keeps Georgia Women Alive."

82   referred to Lynch as . . . way I can put it.": Dijana Kunovac, "A Momma's Boy," *Dawg Post.com*, April 27, 2011, http://georgia.scout.com/2/1067793.html.

82   "When we were young, . . . me become a man,": Kunovac, "A Momma's Boy."

82   My life would have been . . . in a bad or good way.: Kunovac, "A Momma's Boy."

83   the company decided to . . . response was more airborne bovines.: Garbin, p. 224.

83   "it appeared that any fan . . . flung it onto the field," Garbin, p. 225.

83   On a night when . . . a triumphant Georgia team.: Garbin, p. 225.

84   When UGA offensive coordinator . . . has ever seen that before.": Marc Weiszer, "Buldogs Click in Five-Wide-Receiver Set," *DOGbytesonline.com*, Oct. 2, 2012, http://dogbytesonline.com/bulldogs-click.

84   It was entirely of . . . throw 35 passes in a game," Loran Smith, *Wally's Boys*, p. 14.

84   35 passes amounted to half . . . way ahead of them.": Loran Smith, *Wally's Boys*, p. 15.

84   We had the west coast offense at Georgia in 1939. Loran Smith, *Wally's Boys*, p. 14.

84   'the ultimate role model for all loyal UGA alumni': "William C. 'Bill Hartman," www.uga.edu/gm/artman/publish/printer_0606_hartman.html.

85   he posted a trick shot . . . net from the stands.": Tim Tucker, "'This Kid Got Us into 10 Million Homes,'" *UGA sports blog*, March 5, 2010, http://blogs.ajc.com/uga-sports-blog/2010/03/05.

85   "Back-to-back, jack,": Tim Tucker, "Fox Trumps Richt," *UGA sports blog*,

Feb. 28, 2010, http://blotgs.ajc.com/uga-sports-blog/2010-02-28.

85   "I woke up the other . . . It's been great publicity.": Tucker, "'This Kid Got Us.'"

85   As Barkley looked on . . . that's why it rocks,": Tucker, "'This Kid Got Us.'"

85   This kid got us into 10 million homes.: Tucker, "'This Kid Got Us.'"

86   When he was 12, Walker . . . number of unspeakable acts to possess.": Terry Todd, "'My Body's Like An Army.'"

86   Johnson County High in Wrightsville . . . in the weight room that fall.: Todd, "'My Body's Like An Army.'"

86   He was strength tested with . . . thousand-dollar mule, why tempt fate?": Todd, "'My Body's Like An Army.'"

86   Soon as I don't . . . a good weight program.: Todd, "'My Body's Like An Army.'"

87   "the best hire [Vince Dooley] ever made.": Hix, *Stadium Stories* (Guilford, CN: The Globe Pequot Press, 2006), p. 4.

87   Russell was a stern . . . a wall for that guy,": Hix, *Stadium Stories*, p. 5.

87   He called Roger Dancz, the . . . did something exceptional.: "Erk Russell," *Wikipedia the free encyclopedia*, en.wikipedia.org/wiki/Erk_Russell.

87   he would but his players' . . . down the coach's face.: Hix, *Stadium Stories*, p. 5.

87   I scabbed my head up in . . . It became a tradition.: Hix, *Stadium Stories*, p. 5.

88   "for his unparalleled contributions to the Bulldog athletic program.": "Dan Magill," *Wikipedia, the free encyclopedia*, en.wikipedia.org/wiki/Dan_Magill.

88   Early on, Magill gained . . . sports editor Ed Danforth.: Magill, *Dan Magill's Bull-Doggerel* (Atlanta: Longstreet Press, 1993), p. 163.

88   At high noon before . . . carriage bells rang,: Magill, *Dan Magill's Bull-Doggerel*, p. 164.

88   Magill was sure he had . . . the national competition.: Magill, *Dan Magill's Bull-Doggerel*, p. 165.

88   I only used two : . . . my right forefinger.: Magill, *Dan Magill's Bull-Doggerel*, p. 165.

89   Greene said that after . . . confident Georgia could score.: Garbin, *"Then Vince said to Herschel . . .*", p. 232.

89   They are just too much for Georgia right now.: Suggs, *Top Dawg*, p. 5.

90   "Ever since I could . . . to play in the WNBA,": Roger Clarkson, "Trio of Lady Bulldogs Fulfill [sic] Dreams," *DOGbytesonline.com. Athens Banner-Herald.* 16 April 2013.

90   "Growing up, I think . . . to play professionally.": "Three Lady Bulldogs Selected in WNBA Draft," *georgiadogs.com*, April 15, 2013, http://www.georgiadogs.com/sports/w-baskbl/spec-rel/041513aab.html.

90   "It's just a blessing from God,": "Three Lady Bulldogs Selected."

90   "I just thanked God" . . . "I felt really blessed,": Clarkson, "Trio of Lady Bulldogs."

90   You think about it . . . hear your name called.: "Three Lady Bulldogs Selected."

91   Pennington arrived in Athens . . . bigger than his left.: Loran Smith, "Durward Pennington Kicked Way into UGA History." *DOGbytesonline.com*, March 8, 2013, http://dogbytesonline.com/loran-smith-durward-pennington.

91   "upright,, square-toe-shoed, straight-on" kicker: Loran Smith, "Durward Pennington."

91   with its long, swinging leg action.: Loran Smith, "Durward Pennington."

91   [Today's kickers] would view . . . honored by a history museum.: Loran Smith, "Durward Pennington."

92   Robinson "has definitely been . . . people celebrate that enough.": Chip Towers, "Ideal Student-Athlete Christian Robinson Not Quite Ready for Graduation," *UGA sports blog*, Dec. 13, 1012, http://blogs.ajc.com/uga-sports-blog/2012/12/13/ideal-student-athlete-christian-robinson.

92   "If I could stay . . . I love it here.": Towers, "Ideal Student-Athlete."

92   Coach Richt tells you . . . before you know it.": Towers, "Ideal Student-Athlete."

BULLDOGS

BIBLIOGRAPHY

Arnzen, Chris. "Alec Millen: From the NFL Field to the Mission Field: The Testimony of a Former New York Jet & San Francisco 49er." *Iron Sharpens Iron*. 19 Nov. 2008. sharpens.blogsports.com/2008/11/mp3-available-here_19.html.

Asher, Gene. "Meet 'Mr. Nice Guy.'" *Georgia Trend*. Nov. 2004. www.georgiatrend.com/November-2004/meet-mr-nice-guy.

"Bad at Everything But Winning." *Sports Illustrated*. 19 Sept. 1966. http://vault.sportsillustrated.cnn.com/vault/article/magazine/MAG1079032/index.htm.

Barnhart, Tony. *Always a Bulldog: Players, Coaches, and Fans Share Their Passion for Georgia Football*. Chicago: Triumph, Books, 2011.

-----. *What It Means to Be a Georgia Bulldog: Vince Dooley, Mark Richt, and Georgia's Greatest Players*. Chicago: Triumph Books, 2004.

Bernarde, Scott. "UGA Equestrian Team Set to Defend National Title." *ajc.com*. 25 March 2010. http://www.ajc.com/sports/uga/uga-equestrian-team-set-403630.html.

Bradley, Ken. "Georgia's Todd Gurley Drawing Early Comparisons to Herschel Walker." *Sporting News*. 3 Oct. 2012. aol.sportingnews.com/ncaa-football/story/2012-10-03/todd-gurley-georgia.

Branch, Jonathan. "Fooball Notebook: QB Murray Gets First Win over a Top 10 Opponent." *DOGbytesonline.com*. 27 Oct. 2012. http://dogbytesonline.com/football-notebook-gb-murray-gets-first-win-over-a-top-10-opponent.

Bruce, Robert. "College Running Back Turned Pro Golfer?" *Game Under Repair*. 16 Feb. 2009. gameunderrepair.wordpress.com/2009/02/16/college-football-back-turned-pro-golfer/.

Cabell, Beau. "UGA's Andrews Isn't the Tallest Center, But He Is Learning the Ropes." *Macon Telegraph*. 4 Aug. 2012. http://www.macon.com/2012/08/04/212300/ugas-andrews-isnt-the-tallest.html.

Clarkson, Roger. "Big Man, Big Plans: John Jenkins Brings Size, Personality to D-Line." *DOGbytesonline.com*. 19 Oct. 2012. http://dogbytesonline.com/big-man-big-plans.

-----. "Cornerback Cuff Doesn't Boast About Dogs' Fastest 40 Time." *OnlineAthens.com*. 9 Aug. 2010. http://www.onlineathens.com/stories/080910/foo_692591872.shtml.

-----. "Dogs' Gentle Giant." *DOGbytesonline.com*. 9 Aug. 2011. http://dogbytesonline.com/dogs-gentle-giant-47490.

-----. "Dogs Prevail as Hogs Pitcher Plunks Cone." *DOGbytesonline.com*. 2 May 2011. http://dogbytesonline.com/dogs-prevail-as-hogs-pitcher-plunks-cone-45248/.

-----. "Four-Run Sixth Inning Lifts Georgia over Auburn in Opener." *DOGbytesonline.com*. 4 May 2012. http://dogbytesonline.com/four-run-sixth-inning-lifts-georgia.

-----. "James' Putback Sends Lady Dogs to Sweet 16." *DOGbytes.online.com*. 22 March 2011. http://dogbytesonline.com/james-putback-sends-lady-dogs-to-sweet-16-43870.

-----. "Lady Dogs Prevail in OT." *DOGbytesonline.com*. 4 Feb. 2011. http://dogbytesonline.com/lady-dogs-prevail-in-ot-42000.

-----. "Trio of Lady Bulldogs Fulfill [sic] Dreams, Drafted to WNBA." *DOGbytesonline.com*. *Athens Banner-Herald*. 16 April 2013.

-----. "UGA's Earls on Road to Recovery." *OnlineAthens.com*. 4 July 2011. http://onlineathens.com/stories/070411/gym_85236044.shtml.

---. "Whirlwind of Changes Accompanies Stemke." *OnlineAthens.com*. 27 Jan. 2011. onlineathens.com/stories/012711/vol_776679438.shtml.

Conn, Jordan. "Dogged Pursuit: Jarvis Jones Went from USC to UGA to the Top of NFL Draft Boards." *ESPN the Magazine*. 4 Oct. 2012. http://espn.go.com/college-football/story/_/id/8448679/georgia-bulldogs-lb-jarvis-jones.

Conrad, Andrew. "Years Later, Colt Fans Still Seek Out Art DeCarlo." *explorehowardcom*. 4 May, 2011. http://archives.explorehoward.com/

news/83979/year-later.

Cromartie, Bill. *Clean Old-Fashioned Hate*. Huntsville, AL: The Strode Publishers, Inc., 1977.

"Curran Returns to Native Land after 22 Long Years of Waiting." *DOGbytesonline.com*. *Athens Banner-Herald*. 26 April 2011.

Curtis, Brian. "Faith in the Game." *Echoes of Georgia Football*. Ken Samelson, ed. Chicago: Triumph Books, 2006. 133-152.

"Dan Magill." *Wikipedia, the free encyclopedia*. en.wikipedia.org/wiki/Dan_Magill.

Dooley, Vince. *Dooley's Playbook: The 34 Most Memorable Plays in Georgia Football History*. Athens: Hill Street Press, 2008.

Dooley, Vince with Blake Giles. *Vince Dooley's Tales from the 1980 Georgia Bulldogs*. Champaign, IL: Sports Publishing L.L.C., 2005.

Dooley, Vince with Loran Smith. *Dooley's Dawgs: 40 Years of Championship Athletics at the University of Georgia*. Atlanta: Longstreet Press, 2003.

Doster, Rob and Kevin Daniels, eds. *Game Day Georgia Football*. Chicago: Triumph Books, 2005.

Emerson, Seth. "Former Georgia Kicker Blair Walsh Experiencing Remarkable Turnaround in NFL Rookie Year." *Ledger-Enquirer*. 12 Jan. 2013. http://www.ledger-enquirer.com/2013/01/12/234126/former-georgia-kicker-blair-walsh.html.

Erk Russell. *Wikipedia, the free encyclopedia*. en.wikipedia.org/wiki/Erk_Russell.

"Football Notebook: Special Teams Flirt with Disaster; King, Mitchell Have Huge Nights." *DOGbytesonline.com*. 20 Oct. 2012. http://dogbytesonline.com/football-notebook-special-teams-flirt-with-disaster.

Garbin, Patrick. *"Then Vince Said to Herschel . . .": The Best Georgia Bulldog Stories Ever Told*. Chicago: Triumph Books, 2007.

Harris, J. Gerald. "Katharyn Richt: Preseason and Postseason #1-Ranked Mom." *The Christian Index*. 7 May 2009. http://www.christianindex.org/5431.article.

Higgins, Ron. "SEC Traditions: Bobo Knows How to 'Bowl' Them Over." *SEC Digital Network*. 29 Dec. 2010. http://www.secdigitalnetwork.com/SECNation/SECTraditions/tabid/1073/Article/218349.

-----. "SEC Traditions: It was Always Easy Being Greene." *SEC Digital Network*. 27 Sept. 2012. http://www.secdigitalnetwork.com/SECNation/SECTraditions/tabid/1073/Article/237353.

------. "SEC Traditions: Pollack Is Still a Showstopper." *SEC Digital Network*. 9 Dec. 2011. http://www.secdigitalnetwork.com/SECNation/SECTraditions/tabid1073/Article/229991.

-----. "SEC Traditions: The Dooley Family Tree." *SEC Digital Network*. 2 Sept. 2010. http://www.secdigitalnetwork.com/SECNation/SECTraditions/tabid/1073/Article/134279.

-----. "SEC Traditions: UGA VIII." *SEC Digital Network*. 22 Oct. 2010. http://www.secdigitalnetwork.com/SECNation/SECTraditions/tabid/1073/Article/21644.

Hix, Tim. *Stadium Stories: Georgia Bulldogs*. Guilford, CN: The Globe Pequot Press, 2006.

Kunovac, Dijana. "A Momma's Boy." *Dawg Post.com*. 27 April 2011. http://georgia.scout.com/2/1067793.html.

Lancaster, Mark. "No. 3: University of Georgia Athlete of the Century: Frank Sinkwich." Ken Samelson, ed. *Echoes of Georgia Football: The Greatest Stories Ever Told*. Chicago: Triumph Books, 2006. 47-55.

Lidz, Franz. "Mirror, Mirror." *Sports Illustrated*. 15 Nov. 1999. http://sportsillustrated.cnn.com/vault/article/magazine/MAG1017687/index.htm.

MacArthur, John. *Twelve Ordinary Men*. Nashville: W Publishing Group, 2002.

Magill, Dan. "Bulldogs' Zippy Morocco Shocked Vols in Knoxville in 1953. *OnlineAthens.com*. 23 Feb. 1999. onlineathens.com/stories/022399/dog_022399032.shtml.

-----. *Dan Magill's Bull-Doggerel: Fifty Years of Anecdotes from the Greatst Bulldog Ever*. Atlanta: Longstreet Press, 1993.

-----. "Lawrence Deserving of Cotton Bowl Hall of Fame." *OnlineAthens.com*. 27 Jan. 2003.

onlineathens.com/stories/012703/dog_20030127027.shtml.

"Mark Fox Profile." www.georgiadogs.com/sports/m-baskbl/mtt/fox_mark00.html.

"Miller Scores Career-High 25 Points to Lead Lady Bulldogs over Wildcats." *DOGbyteson line.com*. 3 Feb. 2013. http://dogbytesonline.com/miller-scores-career-high.

Newberry, Paul. "Capital One Bowl 2004 Georgia 34 Purdue 27." www.mmbolding.com/bowls/Capital_One_2004.htm.

Outlar, Jesse. *Between the Hedges: A Story of Georgia Football*. Huntsville, AL: The Strode Publishers, 1974.

"Rennie Curran." *georgiadogs.com*. http://www.nmnathletics.com/ViewArticledbm/?DB_OEM_ID=88008&ATCLI1.

"Rennie Curran." *Wikipedia, the free encylopedia*. en.wikipedia.org/wiki/Rennie_Curran.

Smith, Loran. "1931 Georgia-Florida Game One for the Books." *DOGbytes.com*. 29 Oct. 2010. http://dogbytesonline.com/smith-1931-georgia-florida-game.

-----. "Athens' Amp Arnold Was Hometown Hero in 1978 Win over Yellow Jackets." *DOG bytesonline.com*. 23 Nov. 2012. http://dogbytesonline.com/loran-smith-athens-amp-arnold.

-----. "Bulldogs' WR Conley a Man of Many Talents." *DOGbytesonline.com*. 23 Feb 2011. http://dogbytesonline.com/smith-bulldogs-wr-conley.

-----. "Durham's Life After a Bulldog Football Player." *georgiadogs.com*. 19 Jan. 2011. http://www.georgiadogs.com/sports/m-footbl/spec-rel/011911aaa.html.

-----. "Durward Pennington Kicked Way into UGA History." *DOGbytesonline.com*. 8 March 2013. http://dogbytesonline.com/loran-smith-durward-pennington.

-----. "Georgia Caps Season with Nearly Everything Clicking." *DOGbytesonline.com*. 7 Jan. 2013. http://dogbytesonline.com/loran-smith-georgia-caps-season.

-----. "Jones' Performance Against Florida Best All-Time in Series." *DOGbytesonline.com*. 30 Oct. 2012. http://dogbytesonline.com/loran-smith-jarvis-jones-performance.

-----. *Wally's Boys*. Athens: Longstreet Press, 2005.

-----. "Zippy Morocco Celebrates 60 Years." *GeorgiaDogs.com*. 28 Feb. 2013. www.georgia dogs.com./sports/m-baskbl/spec-rel/022813aaa.html.

Starrs, Chris. "UGA Snappe Frix Has a Story to Tell from His Climb from Walk-On to Starter." *DOGbytesonline.com*. 29 Dec. 2012. http://dogbytesonline.com/uga-snapper-frix-has-a-story-to-tell.

Suggs, Rob. *Top Dawg: Mark Richt and the Revival of Georgia Football*. Nashville: Thomas Nelson, 2008.

"Three Lady Bulldogs Selected in WNBA Draft." *georgiadogs.com*. 15 April 2013. http://www.georgiadogs.com/sports/w-baskbl/spec-rel/041513aab.html.

Todd, Terry. "'My Body's Like an Army.'" *Sports Illustrated*. 4 Oct. 1982. http://sports illustrated.cnn.com/vault/article/magazine/MAG1125982/index.htm.

Towers, Chip. "Georgia's Marlon Brown: 'Never Unlucky, Never Unfortunate, Just Blessed.'" *UGA sports blog*. 30 Dec. 2012. http://blogs.ajc.com/uga-sports-blog/2012/12/30/georgias-marlon-brown.

-----. "Ideal Student-Athlete Christian Robinson Not Quite Ready for Graduation." *UGA sports blog*. 13 Dec. 2012. http://blogs.ajc.com/uga-sports-blog/2012/12/13/ideal-student-athlete-christian-robinson.

Tucker, Tim. "Former Walk-On McPhee Living His Dream as a Dog." *The Atlanta Journal-Constitution*. 10 March 2010. http://www.ajc.com/sports/uga/former-walk-on-mcphee-361152.html.

-----. "Fox Trumps Richt, Makes Sports Center 'Top 10' with Trick Shot." *UGA sports blog*. 28 Feb. 2010. http://blogs.ajc.com/uga-sports-blog/2010/02/28.

-----. "'This Kid Got Us into 10 Million Homes,' Mark Fox Says of Walk-on Connor Nolte." *UGA sports blog*. 5 March 2010. http://blogs.ajc.com/uga-sports-blog/2010-03-05.

-----. "Who's Top Dog All-Time in Games Played? Tavarres King, UGA Says."

UGA sports blog. 24 Dec. 2012. http://blogs.ajc.com/uga-sports-blog/2012/12/24/whos-top-dog-all-time-in-games-played.

Weiszer, Marc. "Bulldogs Click in Five-Wide-Receiver Set." *DOGbytesonline.com*. 2 Oct. 2012. http://dogbytesonline.com/bulldogs-click.

-----. "Bulldogs Reach 20 Wins with Rout of Tigers." *OnlineAthens.com*. 3 March 2011. http://onlineathens.com/stories/03011/mens_793737967.shtml.

-----. "Capital W: Murray's 5 TDs Lift Georgia Past Nebraska." *DOGbytesonline.com*. 1 Jan. 2013. http://dogbytesonline.com/capital-w.

-----. "Dogs Showed 'Mental, Physical Toughness' in Win over Mizzou." *DOGbytesonline.com*. 9 Sept. 2012. http://dogbytesonline.com/dogs-showed-mental-physical-toughness-in-win-over-mizzou.

----- "Durham 'Speechless' in Seattle." *OnlineAthens.com*. 1 May 2011. http://onlineathens.com/stories/05011/foo_822578051.shtml.

-----. "Fox Has Strong Ties, Fond Memories of Time Spent at Washington." *OnlineAthens.com*. 16 March 2011. http://onlineathens.com/stories/031611/men_800334874.shtml.

-----. "Kowase Keeps Georgia Women Alive in NCAA Tourney." *DOGbytesonline.com*. 12 May 2012. http://dogbytesonline.com/kowase-keeps-georgia-women-alive.

-----. "Mizzou DT Gets in First Verbal Jabs; Richt Calls Matchup 'a Huge Game.'": *DOGbytesonline.com*. 2 Sept. 2012. http://dogbytesonline.com/mizzou-dt-gets-in-first-verbal-jabs.

-----. "Quick Hits: Dawson Yet to Meet with NCAA; Richt's Mother Asks about 'Old Man Football.'" *DOGbytesonline.com*. 5 Sept. 2012. http://dogbytesonline.com/quick-hits-dawson-yet-to-meet.

-----. "'Test of Toughness': Aaron Murray Working to Get Back on Right Track Against Ole Miss." *DOGbytesonline.com*. 31 Oct. 2012. http://dogbytesonline.com/test-of-toughness.

-----. "Welcome to the SEC: No. 7 Georgia Spoils Missouri's Conference Debut." *DOGbytesonline.com*. 9 Sept. 2012. http://dogbytesonline.com/welcome-to-the-sec.

-----. "Wild Escape: Georgia Holds Off Kentucky; QB Murray Has Record Night." *DOGbytesonline.com*. 20 Oct. 2012. http://dogbytesonline.com/wild-escape.

White, Chris. "UGA Coaches Go Out of Their Way to Avoid Jinxing Swafford." *DOGbytesonline.com*. 6 May 2012. http://dogbytesonline.com/uga-coaches-go-out-of-their-way-to-avoid-jinxing-swafford-57896.

"William C. 'Bill' Hartman." www.uga.edu/gm/'artman/publish/printer_0606_hartman.html.

Wolk, Ben. "Blast from the Past: Senior Kicker Walsh Felt 'Like Old Times' in Final Home Game." *The Red & Black*. 19 Nov. 2011. http://www.redandblack.com/sports/blast-from-the-past-senior-kicker-Walsh.

Yoculan, Suzanne & Bill Donaldson. *Perfect 10: The University of Georgia GymDogs and the Rise of Women's College Gymnastics in America*. Athens: Hill Street Press, 2006.

BULLDOGS

INDEX
(LAST NAME, DEVOTION DAY NUMBER)

203